A Farm Journal Craft Book

MORE SCRAP SAVER'S
STITCHERY

SANDRA LOUNSBURY FOOSE

Farm Journal, Inc.
Philadelphia, Pennsylvania

Distributed to the trade by
Doubleday & Company, Inc.
Garden City, New York

Other Farm Journal Craft Books

Scrap Saver's Stitchery Book (by Sandra Lounsbury Foose)
Let's Make a Patchwork Quilt
Farm Journal's Homespun Christmas
Farm Journal's Design-and-Sew Children's Clothes
Easy Sewing with Knits
Modern Patchwork

Grateful acknowledgment is made for permission to reprint the following:

Little People Dolls, used by permission from the December, 1972 issue of
Good Housekeeping magazine. Copyright © 1972 by The Hearst Corporation.

Farmer Bunny Family in a Carrot, used by permission from the August, 1978
issue of *Redbook* magazine. Copyright © 1978
by The Redbook Publishing Company.

Christmas Tote Bag and Ornaments, Angel and Santa Wreaths, Noel Banner,
all reproduced by permission from *Good Ideas for Decorating* magazine from
Armstrong. Copyright © 1978, 1979, 1980 by Armstrong World Industries, Inc.

Pattern Art: Sandra Lounsbury Foose

Book Design: Michael P. Durning

Photography: Fred Carbone;
except pages 103, 113, 116, courtesy
Good Ideas for Decorating.

Library of Congress Cataloging in Publication Data

Foose, Sandra Lounsbury.
  More scrap saver's stitchery.

  (Farm journal craft books)
  1. Needlework.   2. Handicraft.   I. Title.
II. Series.
TT760.F66   746.4   81-238
ISBN 0-385-17526-4   AACR2

Contents

INTRODUCTION   1

DESIGNS FOR ANYTIME

Bear Nap Mat   3
Lovable Lions   9
Little People Dolls   14
Piggy Laundry Bag   19
Watermelon Hat and Pockets   24
Road Rug   26
Pinup Pincushions   28
Farmer Bunny Family in a Carrot   35
Crayon Friends   45
Saturday Morning Sackhound   54
Cradle Diaper Bag with Teddy Toy   59
Potholders   64
Cozy Quilt   70
Kitchen Kittens   81
Mosaic Patchwork Pillows   86
Puzzle Placemat   88

ESPECIALLY FOR CHRISTMAS

Christmas Placemats   92
Santa Stocking   98
Noel Banner   103
Angel and Santa Wreaths   117
Christmas Tote Bag & Ornaments   122

HOW-TO SECTION   129

From One Scrap Saver to Another

Once upon a time, a long time ago, the inspiration for all my scrap stitchery came from fabric odds and ends I had saved in a neat little scrap bag. My scrap collection quickly outgrew the bag and soon overflowed a large wicker picnic basket as well. I started stuffing pieces into a drawer, then another drawer, and then another. Today the assortment fills two huge antique steamer trunks in my attic and various cardboard boxes, and it's *still* growing! Does that sound like you?

I can't seem to walk past a fabric shop without checking for just one more good green floral or a new blue geometric print. It's habit-forming! Over the years, I've developed a virtual fabric library, and within each trunk the "scrap bags" have become individual color bags holding separate bundles of solids, checks, stripes, etc.

Yes, it's hard to stop once you've started searching, salvaging, and storing fabrics. But this is really a first-rate *good* habit, I think, because you always have such a great source of inspiration right at your fingertips. The resources are all within your reach to create a quick and silly gift or a lovely piece of heirloom handwork.

As you use this book, I hope you will find many of the necessary supplies and materials tucked away in your scrap bags, baskets, boxes or trunks. At the end of the book in the How-to Section, I've made suggestions for helpful techniques and equipment; please do check that section before you begin any project.

I think most people will probably use my book for just the patterns, but it's my hope that the ideas presented will actually be a starting point for you. I'm hopeful you'll be inspired to find new uses for the patterns given here. Or, better yet, perhaps you'll find the courage to depart from my material and create something uniquely your own.

Making a handmade gift is a loving gesture. I'm sure you'll agree that it's quite different from buying something ready-made in a store, no matter how thoughtful your selection. The gift you make yourself enriches you, the maker, as well as the person who receives, appreciates and uses it. In a sense, you both receive a gift.

This book was written for all scrap savers, and it's dedicated to you—because you're special. I know this for a fact because my first book, *Scrap Saver's Stitchery Book,* introduced me to a number of scrap savers. I saw them in person at author's luncheons, library teas, and club meetings, and occasionally I met them through phone calls and warm friendly letters. Sometimes they even sent me photographs of their families and their state fair blue ribbons! At times, much to my delight, they sent me beautiful samples of their own innovative handwork. So, this book is for them—and for you.

It's for you who generously give so much of your precious time to make treasures for church and school bazaars. It's for you who sew patches on patches to save a love-worn soft toy. It's for you who somehow make room in your busy days to create lovely handmade gifts and surprises. It's for you who patiently teach funny little hands to cut and sew while you answer so many questions!

You have done so much for others—you should have a book dedicated to you!

Sandy Foose

1

I made this cozy companion for my little daughter when she was about a year old. At that time, she was a friend of all bears and, indeed, "Beah!" was one of her first words. I intended this bear to be a "wrap around," but she wanted it for a "drag around." It followed her all over the house, collecting dust balls in its wake. We now use it for a rug in a corner of her room.

If you want to make this specifically for a rug, you can cut it from washable, trim-to-fit bathroom carpeting so it will have a slip-resistant backing. In this case, omit the gingham backing. A 4x6' piece of carpeting (¾" pile) should yield two bears if you turn their heads and feet in opposite directions when you lay them out. Trace the bear shapes on the rug's latex backing and cut without adding a seam allowance. Sew on the face and you're done!

You can increase the size of the grid as much as you wish to make bigger and bigger bears, but remember that the patterns for facial features should be enlarged, too.

Another use for this pattern would be as an appliqué for a baby quilt. Enlarge the bear to any size you wish. Cut it from a soft, textured fabric, such as velour, flannel, or terry cloth, and appliqué it to a small quilt of printed calico. For this, you'll probably need to use a wide border or ruffle around the quilt to balance the large bear shape.

Bear Nap Mat

(color photo, page 5)

Materials

Washable white fake fur, 36x45"
1 yard red checked gingham (1" checks), 45" wide, for backing
Polyester quilt batting, 36x45" (optional if fake fur is very thick)
Black fabric scrap, 2¼x7½"; black thread
Red fabric scrap, 3¾x7½"; red thread
3 yards black washable yarn
White thread: regular and heavy-duty

Directions

Finished mat is 34x44". Each square on the pattern grid = 2 square inches.

1. On tracing paper or several large paper bags taped together, enlarge pattern for bear; follow directions in How-to Section. On enlarged pattern, cut away nose, eyes, cheeks and mouth to make a template for marking features on fabric.

2. Trace actual-size patterns for nose, eyes and cheeks from book. Cut out patterns. *Pattern lines are stitching lines; add seam allowance when cutting fabric.*

3. Pin bear pattern to wrong side of fake fur and gingham, and trace around outline once on each fabric. Cut out both pieces as well as a matching batting piece, adding ¼" seam allowance all around each shape.

4. Mark placement of eyes, nose, mouth and cheeks on wrong side of fake fur; transfer to front of head, using basting stitches.

5. On wrong side of black fabric, use a white pencil to trace around patterns for eyes and nose. Cut out two eyes and one nose, adding ¼" seam allowance. On wrong side of red fabric, trace and cut two cheeks, adding ¼" seam allowance.

6. To transfer eye, nose and cheek outlines to front of fabrics, make tiny stitches along the pencil lines drawn on the wrong side of the fabric. Clip the seam allowance on each piece, then turn under and baste.

7. Pin features in place on bear head and appliqué by hand; make sure needle goes all the way through to back of fake fur. Use one strand of black yarn to chain-stitch mouth and the line that runs from nose to mouth. (See embroidery stitches in How-to Section.)

8. Layer the bear-shaped pieces in this order: batting; backing (right side up); front (wrong side up). Pin edges together and machine-stitch ¼" from edge, leaving a 6" opening along one leg. Clip curves and into V areas at neck, crotch, arms and ears; trim batting close to seam. Turn right side out and use a blunt tool to poke out edges. Use a sturdy needle to pull the fake fur nap out of any seams where it is caught.

9. Tie mat in a few places with heavy-duty thread to keep fabric layers from shifting. To do this, pass needle and thread from the back through to the front, take a tiny stitch, and return to the back; tie securely.

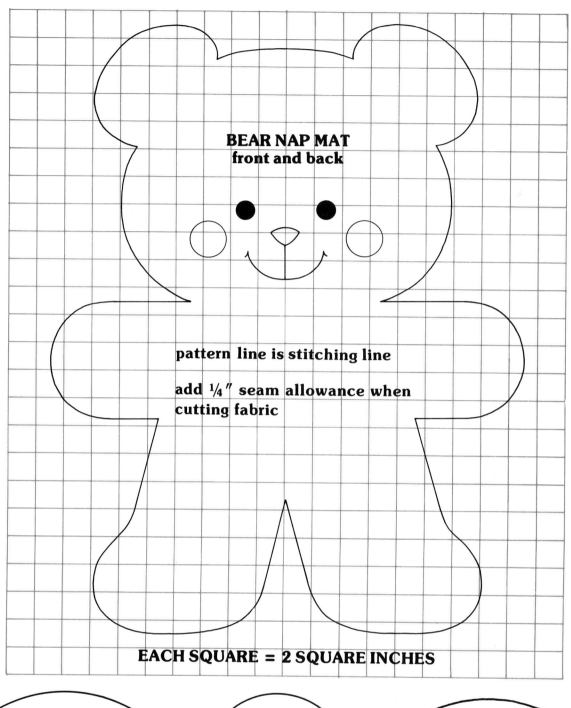

BEAR NAP MAT
front and back

pattern line is stitching line

add ¼″ seam allowance when
cutting fabric

EACH SQUARE = 2 SQUARE INCHES

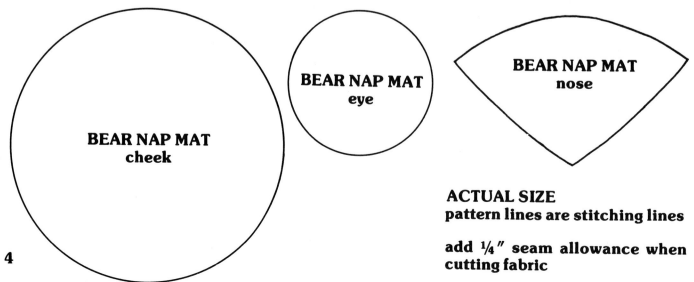

BEAR NAP MAT
cheek

BEAR NAP MAT
eye

BEAR NAP MAT
nose

ACTUAL SIZE
pattern lines are stitching lines

add ¼″ seam allowance when
cutting fabric

Bear Nap Mat is made of fake
fur, backed with gingham in big
checks (see page 3).

Little People Dolls have felt bodies, yarn hair and stitched-on clothes (see page 14).

Every child with toy trucks and autos will love this Road Rug (see page 26).

Tracy Foose (the author's daughter) shows off the Watermelon Hat and Pockets, designed to dress up a simple sundress (see page 24).

Piggy Laundry Bag has a silly grin, a corkscrew tail and a zipper down his back (see page 19).

Here are two lions with two uses! The ruffled-mane lion was designed as a pillow or a soft and cuddly crib toy. A variation on the mane would be to piece it, making use of brightly colored scraps.

The lion with the braided mane is for a door or wall in a child's room. He shares a secret with a little bird friend, who also provides a convenient camou-flage to hide the braid ends.

The bird is very easy to make, and it might be a good design to stitch up in a variety of print scraps for your Christmas tree or bazaar. If you plan to use it as an ornament, remember to add an eye and wing to each side, and perhaps a bow around the neck. At your bazaar, display a flock of these calico bird orna-ments on a bare tree branch.

Lovable Lions

Cuddle Lion Pillow

Materials

Brown scrap, 9x16½"
Brown checked gingham scrap, 7¾x9"
White scrap, 5x13"
Black scrap, 2½x3½"
Brown and white stripe scrap, 6¾x45"
Thread to match fabrics
Embroidery thread: 2½ yards tangerine, 1½ yards black
1¼ yards white medium rickrack
Polyester stuffing

Directions

You'll need a compass for drawing one pattern piece.

1. Patterns are actual size. Trace and cut out patterns for face side, nose strip, nose tip, jowl and ear. Draw a circle, 8⅜" diameter, for head back pattern; mark quarter sections with dots, and cut out. *Pattern lines are stitching lines; add seam allowance when cutting fabric.*

2. Pin patterns to wrong side of fabrics and trace outlines; cut out, adding ¼" seam allowance. From brown fabric, cut one head back, two face sides (one reversed) and two ears (one reversed). From brown checked fabric, cut two ears (one reversed) and one bias nose strip. From white fabric, cut one nose strip (straight of grain) and two jowls (one reversed). From black fabric, cut one nose tip.

3. Transfer marking dots and placement lines to right side of fabric with basting stitches.

4. Use brown and white stripe fabric as is for mane. Fold fabric in half lengthwise, right side out, and press the fold. Open fabric and machine-stitch white rickrack on top of center fold line. Pin short ends of fabric, right sides together, and stitch to form a ring; press seam flat.

5. Refold mane fabric along lengthwise fold, right side out. Press fold line flat along rickrack (only half of rickrack should show on right side). Pin raw edges together and machine-baste ¼" from edge. Mark quarter sections. Pull basting to gath-er mane, then pin and machine-baste mane to right side of head back. (Back of ruffle should lie

against right side of head back, rickrack edge toward center. Pin extra fullness out of way.)

6. Baste white nose strip to back of bias check nose strip and treat as one piece.

7. Pin and stitch a face side piece to each side of nose strip to complete upper face. Clip and press seams flat. (A tailor's ham is helpful for these curved seams.) Make a row of machine stitches on seam line along in-verted curved edge; clip seam al-lowance to stitching.

8. Pin and stitch jowl pieces, right sides together, at center front, stopping stitches at end of pattern outline. (Don't stitch into seam allowance.) Clip and press seam flat.

9. To complete lower face, pin and stitch jowls to nose tip. Keep jowl side up as you work and stitch in two steps, directing both seams toward center of nose. Clip and press seams flat.

10. Spread seam allowance on upper face, and pin section to lower face. Stitch with one continuous line.

11. Pin and stitch each ear front (checked fabric) to back (brown), right sides together; leave bottom edge open. Clip seam or trim with pinking shears. Turn right side out and press flat.

12. Softly fold back of ear forward (on fold line), and pin.

Machine-stitch on seam line of raw edges, and clip to stitching. Spread seam allowance; pin and baste each ear in place on head front. (Checked side of ear should face right side of head, top of ear toward head center.)

13. Pin and stitch head front to back, right sides together, leaving a 3″ opening. Clip around outside, and turn right side out. Stuff pillow, and close opening with hand stitches.

14. Embroider features, using three strands of black embroidery thread. Satin-stitch eyes; chain-stitch eyebrows, mouth, and line from nose to mouth. Use three strands of tangerine to satin-stitch heart-shaped cheeks. (See embroidery stitches in How-to Section.)

ACTUAL SIZE
pattern lines are stitching lines
add ¼″ seam allowance when cutting fabric

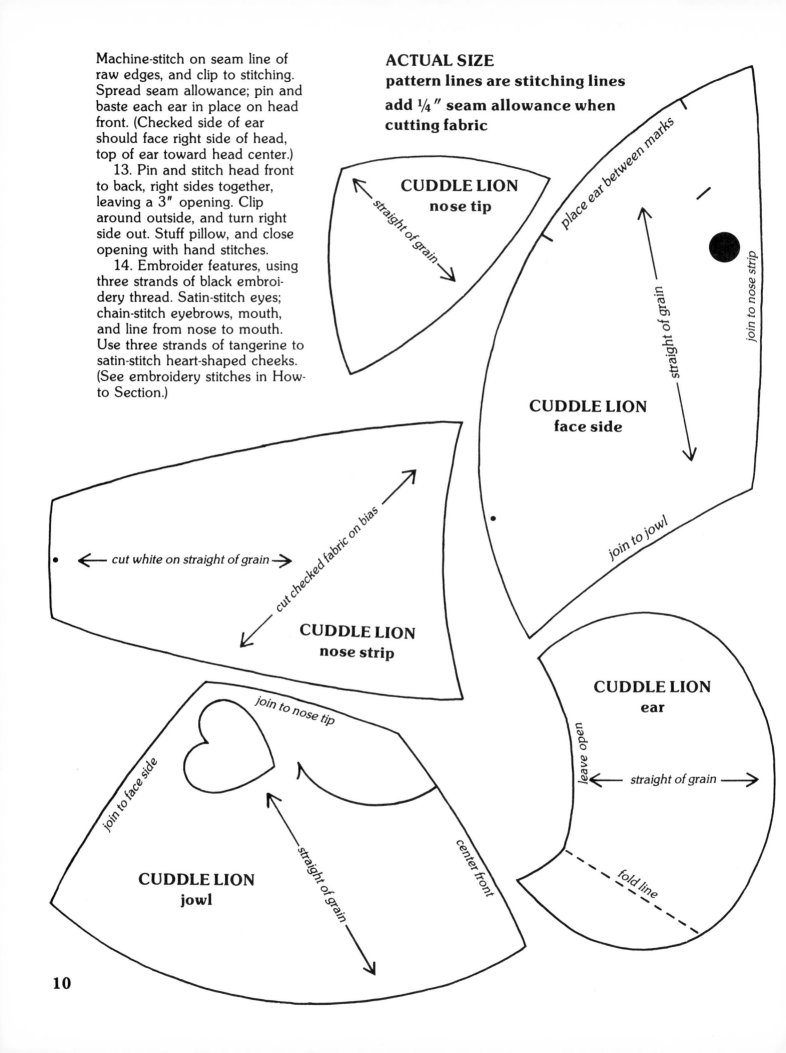

CUDDLE LION
nose tip

straight of grain

place ear between marks

straight of grain

join to nose strip

CUDDLE LION
face side

join to jowl

cut white on straight of grain

cut checked fabric on bias

CUDDLE LION
nose strip

CUDDLE LION
ear

leave open

straight of grain

fold line

join to nose tip

join to face side

center front

straight of grain

CUDDLE LION
jowl

10

Wall Lion
with Braided Mane

Materials

Brown scrap, 13x16"
Brown checked scrap, 8x8"
White scrap, 11½x11½"
Black scrap, 4x4"
Three different brown with white
  prints, 4½x44" each, for mane
Orange with yellow dot scrap,
  4½x7", for bird
Yellow scrap, 3½x3½", for bird
Thread to match fabrics
Embroidery thread: 1 yard black,
  1 yard bright pink
Polyester stuffing
2 shiny black buttons, ⅞" diameter
Plastic curtain ring, ¾" diameter
  (optional)

Directions

You'll need a compass for draw-ing one pattern piece. When cut-ting each 4½x44" strip for mane, try to have one short end on a selvage. (If necessary, you can piece scraps together to make these strips.)

1. Patterns are actual size. Trace and cut out patterns for face side, nose strip, upper and lower nose tip pieces, jowl side, jowl front and ear. Draw a circle, 8" diameter, for head back pat-tern; mark quarter sections with dots, and cut out. *Pattern lines are stitching lines; add seam al-lowance when cutting fabric.*

2. Pin patterns to wrong side of fabric and trace outlines; cut out, adding ¼" seam allowance. From brown fabric, cut one head back, two face sides (one re-versed), and two ears (one re-versed). From brown checked fabric, cut two ears (one re-versed) and one bias nose strip. From white fabric, cut one nose strip (straight of grain), one jowl front and two jowl sides (one re-versed). From black fabric, cut one upper and one lower nose tip piece.

3. Transfer marking dots and placement lines to right side of fabric with basting stitches.

4. Baste white nose strip to back of bias checked nose strip and treat as one piece.

5. On upper nose tip, fold un-der and baste seam allowance of one raw edge; then invisibly ap-pliqué edge to checked nose strip.

6. On lower nose tip, fold un-der and baste seam allowance of both straight edges; then invisibly appliqué edges to jowl front.

7. Pin jowl front to nose strip, right sides together, along the appliquéd edges. Machine-stitch, beginning and ending exactly on the seam line. Layer seam, and cut V s out of seam allowance to eliminate extra fullness. Press seam open.

8. On one face side piece, machine-stitch the inverted curved edge (marked with two short lines); clip into seam allow-ance. Pin this edge to a jowl side (also marked with two short lines), right sides together; stretch seam allowance gently, if neces-sary. Stitch, clip again, and press seam open. Repeat procedure to complete other side section.

9. Pin each side section to the front nose/jowl piece, matching seams. Stitch, clip, and press seams as open as possible.

10. Pin and stitch head front and back, right sides together, leaving seam open about 3". Turn right side out and stuff firmly, molding head as you stuff. Close opening.

11. To make each ear, pin a checked piece to a brown piece, right sides together; stitch around curved edge, leaving bot-tom open. Clip seam allowance or use pinking shears to trim close to stitching. Turn to right side and lightly press. Turn in seam allowance on lower edge, and close with hand stitches.

12. Softly fold ears on fold line, and tack folded edges to-gether at lower edge. Pin and stitch ears in place on head with invisible hand stitches.

13. To make tubes for braids, fold each 4½x44" strip in half lengthwise, right sides together. Stitch a lengthwise seam, ¼" from raw edges, beginning at the selvage edge. Taper seam to-ward fold at other end (see Fig-ure 1). Trim seam allowance to

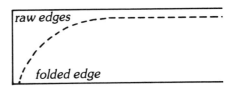

Figure 1   *Stitching tube for braid*

¼" at taper, and clip.

14. Turn each tube right side out and stuff firmly, using a café curtain rod or yardstick. (Selvage at open end is a help.) Tempo-rarily close open ends with string or rubber bands.

15. Tack tapered ends togeth-er securely, and braid mane. Trim ends of tubes if necessary, and re-tie openings so ends of braid are even. Hand-stitch tube ends together securely, mold braid into a ring, and secure with stitches.

16. Insert head, placing braid joint below left ear. Tack head in place on back.

17. Stitch button eyes in place. Using two strands of black embroidery thread, satin-stitch mouth, and chain-stitch eye-brows and line from nose to mouth. (See embroidery stitches in How-to Section.)

18. Trace actual-size patterns for bird body, wing and beak, and cut out.

19. Fold orange dot fabric, right sides together, and trace body once; do not cut out. Fold yellow fabric, right sides togeth-

er. Trace wing once and beak twice (to make four beak pieces); do not cut out.

20. Mark placement dots for openings, and transfer design lines for eye and cheek to right side of fabric. Stitch fabric before cutting, using small machine stitches; leave openings where indicated on wing, beak, head and back. Clip and trim seams, using pinking shears, if possible; cut deeply into V areas at bird neck. Turn all stitched pieces right side out.

21. Lightly stuff bird body and close back opening. Tuck in seam allowance on head, but do not stitch. Fold each beak piece along dotted line shown on pattern. Set one beak unit inside the other at an angle to look like a mouth (see Figure 2), and tack

Figure 2 *Folding fabric to form beak*

together. Insert beak in head, and close opening with invisible stitches. Close opening on wing, and tack wing to right side of bird's body.

22. Using two strands of embroidery thread, satin-stitch a black eye and a pink cheek on bird. Sew bird to lion mane so it hides braid ends.

23. Attach plastic curtain ring to back of mane for hanging, or fashion your own hanging loop from strong string or bias tape.

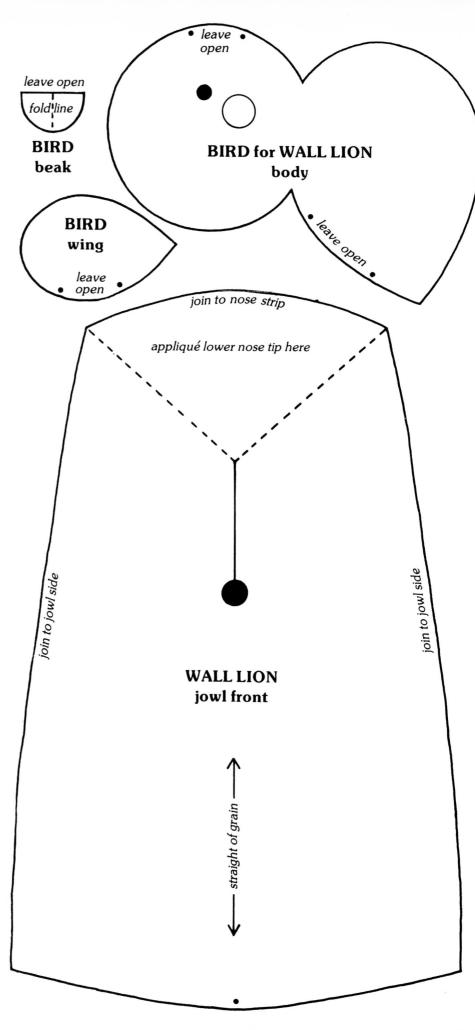

leave open
fold line

**BIRD
beak**

**BIRD
wing**

leave open

• leave
open

**BIRD for WALL LION
body**

leave open

join to nose strip

appliqué lower nose tip here

join to jowl side

join to jowl side

**WALL LION
jowl front**

straight of grain

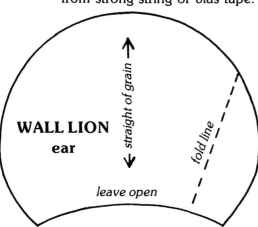

**WALL LION
ear**

straight of grain

fold line

leave open

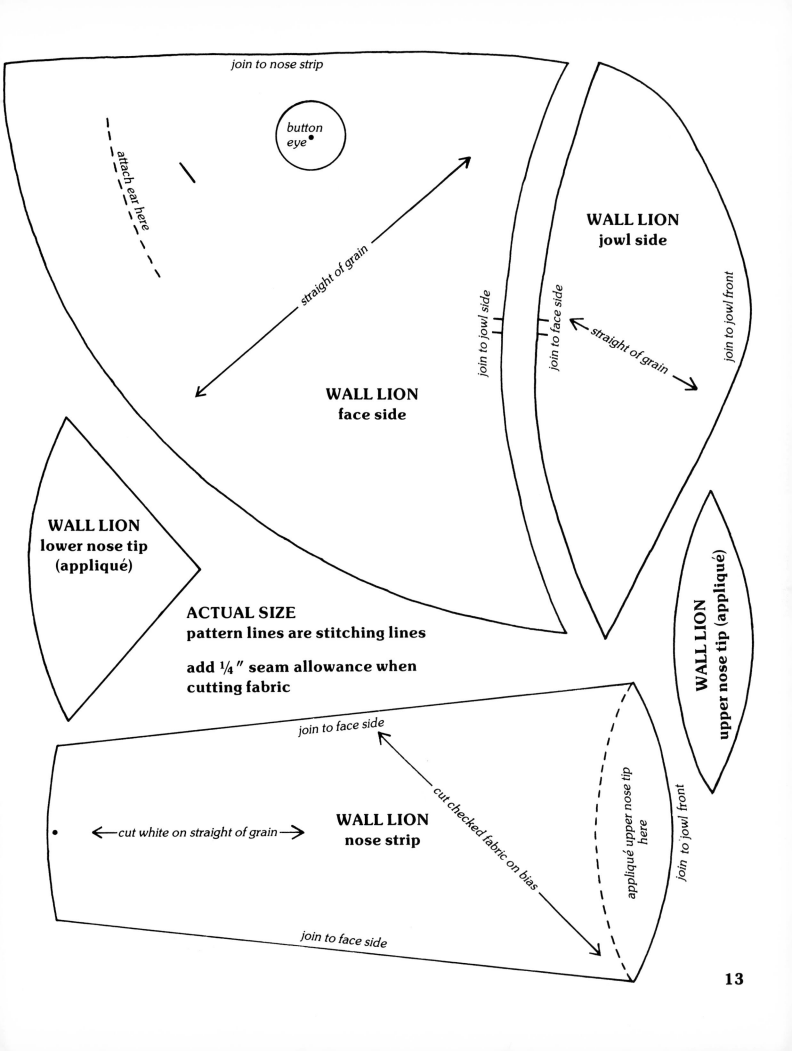

join to nose strip

button
eye •

attach ear here

straight of grain

**WALL LION
face side**

**WALL LION
lower nose tip
(appliqué)**

**ACTUAL SIZE
pattern lines are stitching lines**

**add ¼″ seam allowance when
cutting fabric**

join to jowl side

join to face side

**WALL LION
jowl side**

straight of grain

join to jowl front

**WALL LION
upper nose tip (appliqué)**

join to face side

← cut white on straight of grain →

**WALL LION
nose strip**

cut checked fabric on bias

appliqué upper nose tip here

join to jowl front

join to face side

13

These "little people" dolls are just that—they're playmates for little people. The clothes, shoes, and ribbons are stitched securely in place so all those little pieces don't reappear just at spring cleaning time!

When you sew one of these dolls for a gift, try to make it look like the little person who will play with it. Maybe you can even find fabric that will match some favorite clothing. I added button trims, but if you're making dolls for an "under three" who hasn't yet passed the nibbling stage, do substitute embroidery for the buttons.

You can probably come up with all sorts of variations using the basic patterns. How about doing a little boy doll, covering the whole head with straight hair like that on the front of the bikini doll? Outfit him in overalls or shorts and a T-shirt. You can purchase a tiny buckle and make a grosgrain ribbon belt for him, too.

For a timesaving bazaar idea, make up a few dolls for display, then package and sell your own doll kits. Include mimeographed patterns and instructions.

Fill kit bags with felts and fabrics cut to size, along with the proper yarn, trims and notions. If you do this, buy felt by the yard and cut it to size. Have everyone on the committee donate fabric, felt and trim scraps to make a good variety of kit choices. I would not include the stuffing, because it's difficult to judge the quantity. Any kits you don't sell can be made into finished dolls for another year.

Little People Dolls

Little People Dolls
(color photo, page 6)

General Materials

Felt pieces, 8x9½", two each:
brown, pink or tan
Thread to match felt
Embroidery thread: 1 yard black,
1 yard pink, ½ yard magenta
(substitute pink for black doll)
Polyester stuffing
Long, sharp needle with large eye (to use with yarn for hair)

General Directions

1. Trace and cut out actual-size patterns for doll (on folded tracing paper) and clothing. Dimensions for other clothing pieces are given under directions for individual dolls. *Pattern lines are stitching lines for felt doll; pattern lines are cutting lines for all other fabric and felt pieces.*

2. Use a ball-point pen or soft pencil to trace doll pattern and design lines on one piece of felt, but don't cut out shape until after you stitch it.

Transfer guidelines for top-stitching and facial features to the front of felt with basting stitches. Then pin the two matching pieces of felt, right sides together. Machine-stitch around outline, leaving 1¼" open at top of head for turning.

3. Cut out doll shape about ⅛" from the stitching line, using pinking shears if possible. Clip into V areas at neck and under arms. Slash between legs. Clip curves well if you don't use pinking shears.

Use eraser end of a pencil to invert arms and legs, and turn doll right side out. Stuff doll firmly but keep it rather flat.

4. Close opening. By hand, topstitch evenly along broken lines at shoulder/arm areas and leg tops so arms and legs will bend; use doubled thread. Wrap and tie thread around neck to define head.

5. After adding hair (see individual doll directions), add face. (See embroidery stitches in How-to Section.) Satin-stitch black eyes and pink cheeks, using two strands of embroidery thread. Use a single magenta thread to backstitch mouth. (For visibility, make a pink mouth on black doll.)

Denim Doll

First check list of General Materials for all dolls.

Additional Materials

Blue checked flannel scrap, 7x7"
Blue denim scrap, 6½x10½"
Bandana print scrap, 7¼x7¼"
Beige felt, 5x7", for boot tops
Brown felt, 2½x2¾", for boot soles
White thread
3 yards brown embroidery thread
13 yards ochre yarn (4-ply)
10" white velvet ribbon, ¼" wide
2 small white buttons, ¼" diameter

Directions

1. Follow Steps 1-4 under General Directions.

2. To add hair, thread a large-eyed needle with a 1½-yard length of yarn. Begin at doll front, and use long satin stitches, carrying yarn across head from side seam to center "part" line. Insert needle at center line, and take yarn (inside doll's head) back to side seam.

Work from hairline to top of head, keeping rows even. Also keep yarn tension even (don't pull it too tightly.) Complete one side, then do the other side.

Repeat procedure for back hair, but begin hairline ¾" above the neckline.

3. For each braid, cut three 20" lengths of yarn. Thread needle with one length and pull yarn through eye so that ends meet. Take one stitch at the side of head, pulling yarn halfway

through, then cut needle free. (This should result in four 5" lengths of yarn attached to head.) Repeat with the two other 20" lengths on same side of head to make 12 strands.

Braid yarn to desired length; wrap and tie thread around end of braid. Trim yarn "tails" to desired length.

4. Cut two 5" lengths of narrow velvet ribbon and fold each into a bow shape. Take a stitch at the center, then wrap thread tightly around it a few times to create a bow. Tack a bow to the end of each braid.

5. Embroider face, following Step 5 under General Directions.

6. Trace and cut out two shirt pieces from checked flannel. Right sides together, pin and stitch the underarm seams; leave top open. Clip into V areas under arms and turn shirt right side out.

7. Press under the ¼" seam allowance on sleeve ends and top. Slip shirt over doll's feet and into position. Use invisible hand stitches to close top sleeve seams. Sew edges of neck area and sleeve ends directly to doll.

8. To make overalls, cut two blue denim pant pieces. Press under the ¼" hem allowance at waist and leg bottoms; topstitch ⅛" from folded edges with white thread. Pin pieces, right sides together, and stitch the crotch; trim seam to ⅛" and clip the curve.

Refold so crotch center front and center back seams are lined up, right sides together. Stitch side seams.

9. Turn pants right side out, and put on doll. (You can make a tuck at the back seam to adjust waist if it's too big.)

10. Cut a blue denim bib 1¾x3¼". Press under both short edges and one long edge, and topstitch ⅛" from the edge with white thread.

Cut one long strap ¾x8½", and press under ¼" along both long edges; topstitch down the center with white thread. Cut in half to make two 4¼" short straps. Stitch a small button to each corner of bib top.

11. Tuck bib under pants at front and hand-stitch together at waistline. Tack on straps, crossed in back. Invisibly stitch rest of pants to shirt at waistline.

12. Cut the 7¼" bandana square in half to make two triangles (use just one triangle for scarf). Stitch a ⅛" double hem along each edge. Tie scarf around doll's neck.

13. For each boot, use patterns to cut one brown sole, one beige boot vamp and one beige boot top. Transfer upper boot design to right side of felt by punching through pattern with a large needle, then marking with a ball-point pen. Use two strands of brown embroidery thread to chain-stitch design.

14. Let vamp overlap boot top about ⅛". Join pieces with a blanket stitch, using two strands of brown embroidery thread. Also blanket-stitch top edge of boot.

15. Fit and pin combined boot piece to doll's foot, overlapping edges about ⅛" at back seam. Close with invisible stitches. Pin sole to foot (pins go up vertically into leg). Blanket-stitch sole and boot together with two strands of brown thread. Remove pins.

Bikini Doll

First check list of General Materials for all dolls.

Additional Materials

Terry cloth scrap, 5x8″ (a bargain basement washcloth?)
24″ narrow orange rickrack
30″ orange yarn (or embroidery thread)
1 yard orange velvet ribbon, ¼″ wide
1 yard orange embroidery thread
Orange felt, 2½x5½″
Iron-on fusible web, 2½x2¾″ (or rubber cement)
11½ yards dark brown yarn (4-ply)

Directions

1. Follow Steps 1-4 under General Directions.

2. For hair on back of head, follow Step 2 under Denim Doll. (Hairline begins ¾″ above neckline.) For front bangs, make long satin stitches from top of head down to hairline. Start at center front and work to one side, then work the other side.

3. To make each side ponytail, cut three 12″ lengths of yarn. Thread needle with one length and pull yarn through eye so that ends meet. Take a stitch at side of head, pulling yarn halfway through, then cut needle free. (This should result in four 3″ lengths of yarn attached to head.) Repeat with the two other 12″ lengths on same side of head to make 12 strands.

4. To make velvet ribbon hair bows, follow Step 4 under Denim Doll. Tack a bow to the top of each ponytail.

5. Embroider face, following Step 5 under General Directions.

6. For the bikini bottom, cut a terry cloth strip 1½x8″. Stitch a ¼″ single hem along both long edges, then tack narrow rickrack over the stitching.

Right sides together, stitch the short edges to form a narrow tube. Turn right side out and place on doll, seam at center back. Tack between legs, then tack top edge to doll's waist.

7. For bikini top, use pattern to cut one terry cloth halter; stitch a ¼″ single hem on all edges. Tack rickrack to the upper and lower edges.

Attach orange yarn to each side of top and bottom edges to form ties; cut two neck ties, each 5″ long and two bottom ties, each 7½″ long. Knot cut ends of yarn.

8. Place halter on doll, and tie yarns into bows at neck and lower back. Tack each bow to prevent untying.

9. To make sandals, cut orange felt into two 2½x2¾″ rectangles and join together with iron-on fusible web or rubber cement. (For joining felt, see How-to Section.)

Trace pattern and cut two soles from this double layer of felt. Edge with orange blanket stitches, using six strands of embroidery thread. Pin a sole to the bottom of each foot (pins go up vertically into leg).

10. For each sandal, cut the following lengths of orange velvet ribbon: upper strap, 3¾″; lower strap, 3″; and back strap, 3¼″.

First position and pin (to sole) the top strap to fit foot; tuck ribbon ends between foot and top of sole. Remove sandal and hand-stitch ribbon to upper sole. Return sandal to foot and repeat procedure for lower strap and then for heel strap.

11. Tack sandal to foot between foot and sole. Remove pins.

Party Dress Doll

First check list of General Materials for all dolls.

Additional Materials

Green dotted swiss scrap, 2½x20″
White batiste scrap, 1¾x7¾″
8″ white eyelet ruffle, 1½″ wide
8″ embroidered ribbon, ½″ wide
Lime green felt, 4x5½″
7″ lime green grosgrain ribbon, 5/16″ wide
1 yard lime green embroidery thread
½ yard white patterned lace, 2 5/8″ wide
3 tiny white buttons
1 yard shirred white lace, ¼″ wide
21 yards black yarn (4-ply)

Directions

1. Follow Steps 1-4 under General Directions.

2. To make curly hair, cut a 3-yard length of black yarn and double it in the needle. Starting at the head back, sew small loops over entire head. Try to keep loops fairly uniform and close together.

On the head front, don't bring stitches down to the hairline or you will end up with a very tiny face. Just work the loop stitches toward hairline until it "looks right."

3. For each stocking, cut two patterned lace pieces slightly larger than the leg shape on the doll pattern; use finished edge of lace for back edge of stocking.

4. Working on the back of one leg, pin finished straight edge of lace to back leg seam and stitch it invisibly to doll. Pin-

fit lace over back section of leg and trim; let lace overlap front seam on leg. Then place a lace piece on front of leg, overlapping straight edge at back leg seam.

Leave a little extra seam allowance at leg front seam, turn this under and stitch it invisibly.

5. For underpants, use the 1¾x7¾" white batiste scrap and press under both long edges ¼". Machine-stitch ¼"-wide shirred lace to one long edge. Right sides together, stitch the short ends to form a tube. Turn right side out.

6. Place pants on doll, with seam at the back and lace at the bottom. Tack between legs to make a crotch. Stitch the top edge to doll.

7. Seam ends of eyelet ruffle to make a petticoat. Tack to doll under the arms.

8. For dress bodice, cut two dotted swiss pieces, each 2x3½". (If fabric is too sheer, you can back it with additional batiste.)

On each piece, press under ¼" and stitch the two short edges (armholes) and one long edge (neckline). Invisibly stitch the shirred lace to the three hemmed edges on both bodice pieces. Stitch three tiny buttons to bodice at center front.

9. Position bodice pieces on doll, with lace at neckline. Sew together at shoulders.

10. For the skirt, cut a 2¼x12½" dotted swiss piece. Press under ¼" along one long edge and hem it; add narrow shirred lace to this edge.

Right sides together, make a ¼" seam on the short edges and press flat.

11. Gather raw edge, and place skirt on doll, overlapping bodice raw edges. Pull gathering stitches to fit doll, and tie threads. Baste skirt to bodice. Sew embroidered ribbon around waist, covering raw edge of skirt.

12. For shoes, use patterns to cut soles and tops from green felt. Overlap back seam of each

shoe top ⅛" and stitch together. Blanket-stitch upper edge, using two strands of green embroidery thread. Put shoe top on doll, then pin sole to bottom of foot. Join the two shoe pieces with blanket stitches. Remove pins.

13. To make each shoe bow, cut one 2" length of grosgrain ribbon; fold so ribbon overlaps ⅛" at center. Flatten bow and tack at ribbon center. Cut a 1" tie piece, wrap it around bow center and tack in back. Sew a completed bow to each shoe.

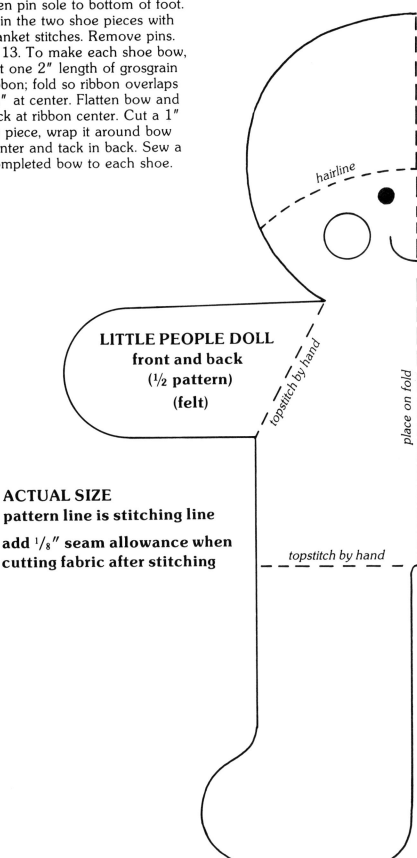

hairline

LITTLE PEOPLE DOLL
front and back
(½ pattern)
(felt)

topstitch by hand

place on fold

ACTUAL SIZE
pattern line is stitching line

add ⅛" seam allowance when cutting fabric after stitching

topstitch by hand

17

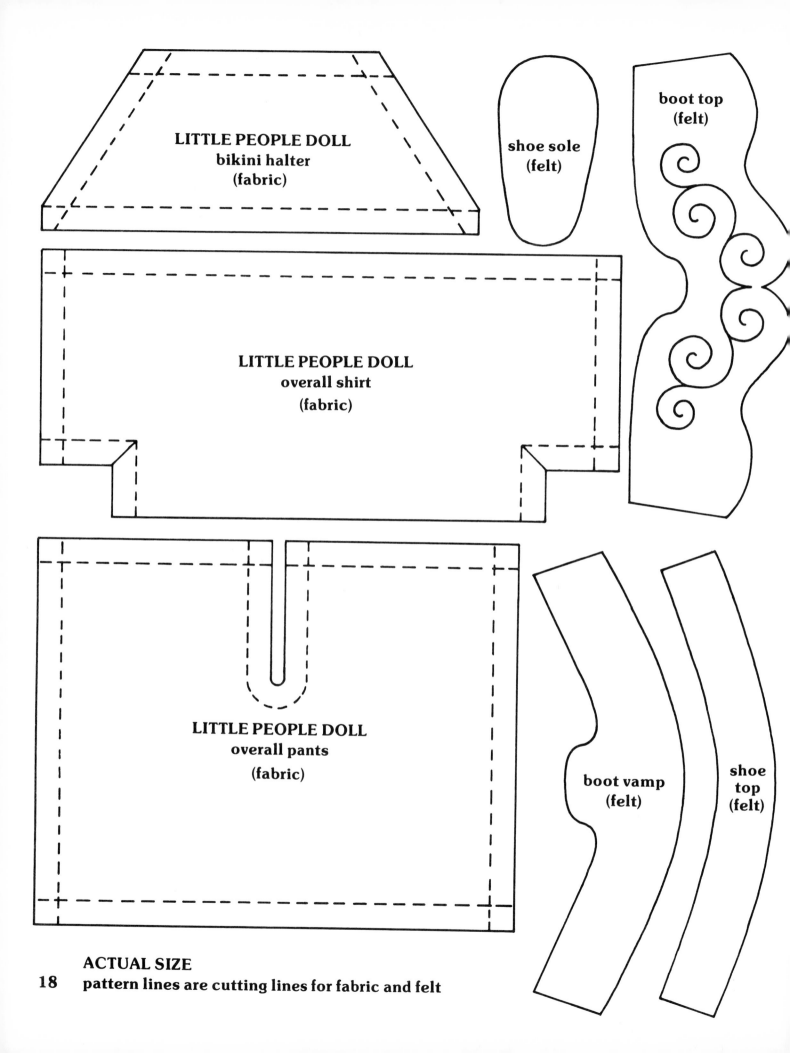

LITTLE PEOPLE DOLL
bikini halter
(fabric)

shoe sole
(felt)

boot top
(felt)

LITTLE PEOPLE DOLL
overall shirt
(fabric)

LITTLE PEOPLE DOLL
overall pants
(fabric)

boot vamp
(felt)

shoe top
(felt)

ACTUAL SIZE

pattern lines are cutting lines for fabric and felt

This little piggy is as soft as a marshmallow and collects dirty clothes for the laundry. Without the handle and zipper, this little piggy can be a puffy pillow toy. It's made of poplin fabric, faced with quilt batting and a lining.

You could make a much simpler and speedier version by using quilted fabric (reversible fabric is nice) and omitting the batting and lining. The result won't be as puffy, but you'll certainly save time. (If you make the quilted fabric version, use unquilted fabric for the tail. Sometimes it's possible to remove the quilting stitches and separate the fabric from the batting.)

This design has a hanging strap, but the pig looks best casually reposed on the floor. The bag would be an appropriate gift for any little people you know who tend to throw their dirty clothes on the floor. Just tell them it's okay, as long as they throw their clothes into the piggy first!

Piggy Laundry Bag

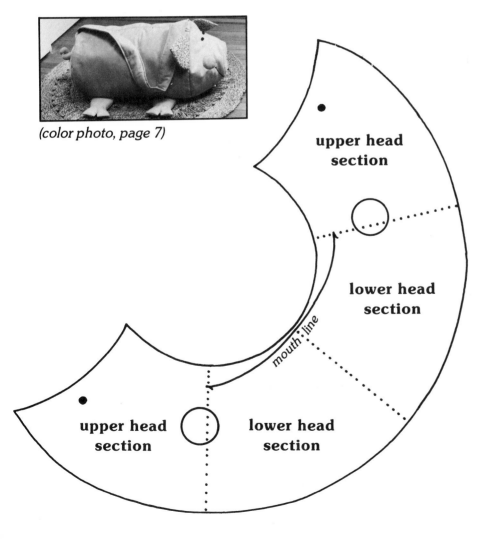

(color photo, page 7)

Figure 1 *Make complete head pattern by tracing upper and lower head sections in position.*

Materials

1¼ yards peach fabric (poplin weight), 44″ wide; matching thread
1 yard pink and orange floral print, 44″ wide, for lining
Brilliant pink scrap (poplin weight), 6x22″; matching thread
Polyester quilt batting, 35x45″
14″ peach zipper
Polyester stuffing
2 brown ball (or half-ball) buttons, ⁷⁄₈″ diameter
3 yards brown embroidery thread

Directions

You'll need a compass for drawing one pattern piece.

1. Trace actual-size patterns for ear, nose, leg and hoof on folded tracing paper. Copy dot mark for quarter section on nose. Cut out shapes, and open paper; add dots to mark center top and center bottom of nose. Trace tail and cheek patterns on single layers of tracing paper, and cut out.

2. Refer to Figure 1 and use a large sheet of tracing paper to make a complete head pattern. Trace actual-size patterns for upper head and lower head sec-

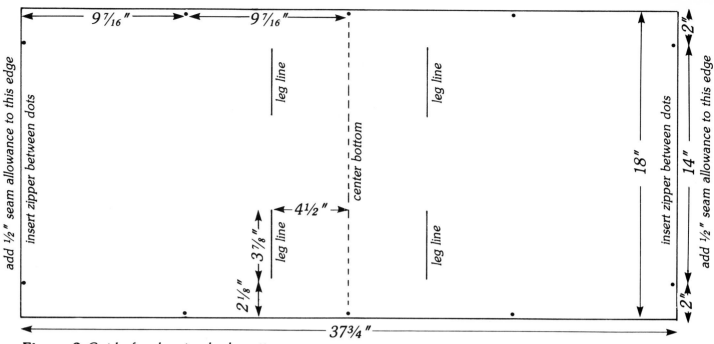

Figure 2 *Guide for drawing body pattern.*

tions, positioning tracing paper so that sections are joined to make one unit. Use dots at edge of pattern to mark the quarter sections, and copy placement lines for features. Cut out complete head pattern.

3. Draw 18x37¾" rectangle for body pattern (see Figure 2). Mark the four leg lines (where legs attach); each line is 3⅞" long, positioned 2⅛" from outside edge of pattern and 4½" from center bottom line. Mark dots on short sides to show zipper placement. Mark dots on long sides to show quarter divisions of pattern. Cut out pattern.

4. Use a compass to make a 12" circle pattern for the backside (see Figure 3). Cut out circle, fold in quarters and mark quarter sections on edge of pattern. Add a 1" circle at center for tail placement.

5. Make pattern for handle by drawing a 5x33" rectangle, using Figure 4 as a guide. Mark center with a broken line, and cut out pattern. *All pattern lines are stitching lines; add seam allowance when cutting fabric.*

6. On wrong side of peach fabric, trace around body pattern, transferring all placement lines. Cut out this piece, adding ½" seam allowance on both short edges (zipper seam) and ¼" seam allowance on both long edges.

7. Also on peach fabric, trace one head, one nose, one backside, one handle, two ears and eight legs. Cut out pieces, adding ¼" seam allowance. Trace tail pattern on wrong side of folded and pinned peach fabric, but don't cut out until tail is stitched. Transfer all placement lines to front of fabric with large basting stitches. (See transfer directions in How-to Section.)

8. On wrong side of print lining fabric, trace around pattern for body. Mark quarter sections by placing dots in the seam al-

pattern lines are stitching lines

add ¼" seam allowance when cutting fabric unless otherwise noted

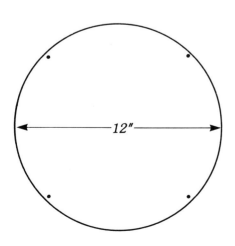

Figure 3 *Guide for drawing backside pattern.*

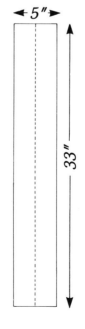

←—5"—→

33"

Figure 4 *Guide for drawing handle pattern.*

20

lowance on right side of fabric. Cut out this piece, adding ½″ seam allowance on both short edges (for zipper) and ¼″ seam allowance on both long edges.

9. Also from print fabric, trace one head, one nose, one backside and two ears. Mark quarter sections on nose and backside with dots placed in seam allowance on right side of fabric. Cut out fabric, adding ¼″ seam allowance to all pieces. Transfer nostrils to front of fabric with basting stitches.

10. On wrong side of brilliant pink fabric, trace two cheeks and eight hoofs. Cut out pieces, with ¼″ seam allowance.

11. Use patterns to cut batting for body, backside, nose and head, adding seam allowance. Pin batting pieces to wrong side of peach pieces, carefully smoothing out wrinkles and lumps. Hand-baste within seam allowance and trim away excess batting.

12. Pin and baste body lining (right side out) to batting, and hand-tack in six or eight places to keep batting from shifting. (Don't let tacks go through to peach fabric.) Pin and baste lining (right side out) to batting on backside, nose and head pieces.

13. Turn under seam allowance on cheeks; pin and appliqué to head, using invisible stitches. Push a little stuffing in as you stitch to make cheeks puffy. Chain-stitch mouth and nostrils, using three strands of brown embroidery thread. (See embroidery stitches in How-to Section.)

14. On head, machine-stitch along seam line of inner curve. (This seam joins the nose.) Pin and stitch head closed at center front; clip seam and press flat.

15. Cut two ears from batting, and pin pieces for each ear together in this order: batting,

peach (right side up), lining (wrong side up). Stitch together, leaving bottom open. Clip off tip and clip curves. Trim batting close to stitching. Turn right side out. Baste lower edge closed without turning in seam allowance, and press lightly.

16. Pin ears to head between dots, with print side of ear against peach side of head. Have raw edges even, with tip of ear toward nose seam. Baste along seam line.

17. On head piece, clip within seam allowance (almost to stitching) all around nose curve; make clips about ¼″ apart. Pin nose in place, matching quarter section dots and gently stretching clipped seam allowance on head. Baste and machine-stitch; clip if necessary.

18. On rectangular body piece, machine-stitch ¼″ from all edges. Pin short edges, right sides together, and machine-stitch each end of zipper seam from raw edge to dot. Machine-baste rest of seam closed (this is a ½″ seam).

19. Center and pin zipper on back of seam, and hand-stitch in place with doubled thread. Finish edge by overcasting zipper tape to lining. Set aside.

20. For handle, cut a piece of batting 2¾x33½″. Pin batting to wrong side of peach handle, with one edge of batting against center line. Invisibly hand-baste batting to center line, catching only one thread of fabric with each stitch. Baste other batting edges to cut edges of fabric with regular basting stitches.

21. Fold handle, wrong side out, along center line and pin. Machine-stitch only the long edge and trim batting close to seam. Turn right side out. Hand-baste along both long sides, with seam exactly on one edge. Machine-topstitch ¼″ from each long edge.

22. Pin handle to body piece, centering it over zipper seam; have raw edges of handle flush with raw edges of body piece.

Machine-stitch ¼″ from edges.

23. Clip seam allowance at open ends of body unit, including handle area; make clips about ¼″ apart and almost to the stitching. Turn body wrong side out and pin backside in place, right sides together. Match quarter section dots and gently stretch clipped seam allowance. Baste, machine-stitch, and clip seam if necessary. Attach head in same manner.

24. Pin a pink hoof to a peach leg, right sides together; stitch and press seam flat. Repeat with remaining legs. Pin two completed hoof/leg pieces, right sides together; stitch, leaving straight edge at top open. Clip curves and into V areas. Trim off corners. Turn right side out and stuff lightly. Complete four legs.

25. Turn under seam allowance on legs, and close with invisible stitches. Use doubled thread and invisible stitches to sew each leg securely to a leg line on body. (Stitches should be on seam edge of leg so leg will be floppy.)

26. To make tail, machine-stitch on curved lines; leave short straight edge open. Trim seam to ¼″ (it will be less in some places). Clip curves and turn tail right side out. Stuff. Turn under ¼″ hem allowance at opening and baste (keep the tail open).

27. Coil tail tightly into corkscrew shape, and tack. Stitch tail invisibly to center of backside.

28. Sew on two button eyes.

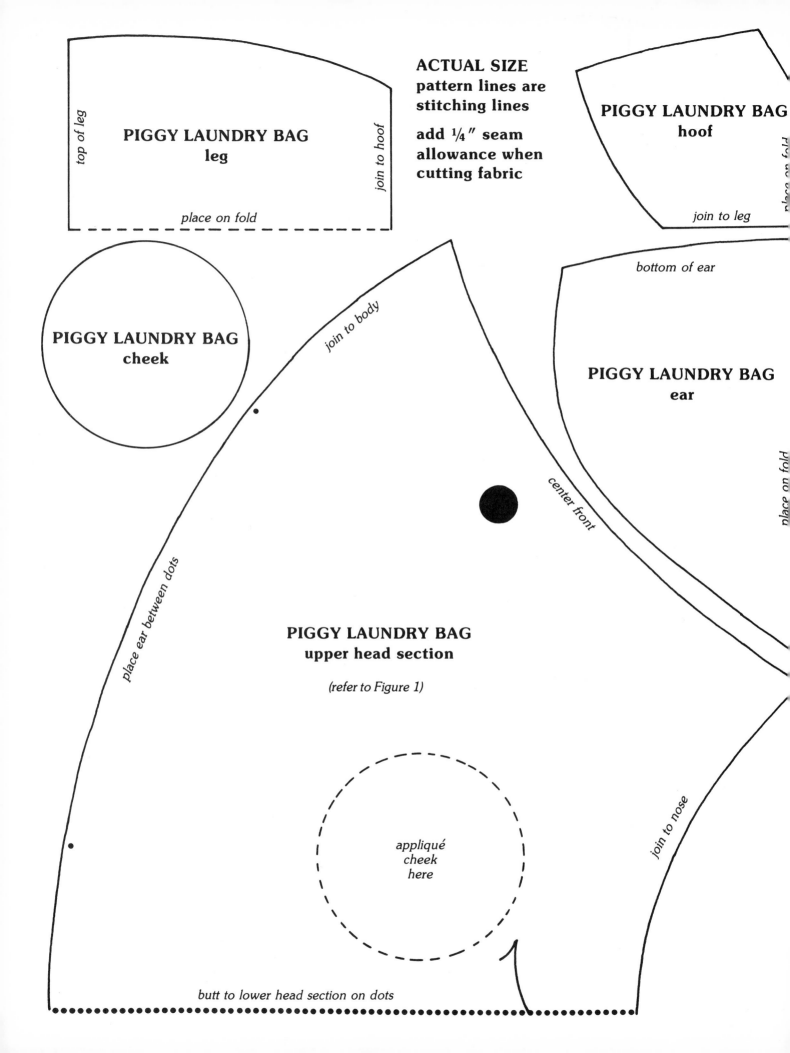

PIGGY LAUNDRY BAG
leg

top of leg

join to hoof

place on fold

ACTUAL SIZE
pattern lines are
stitching lines

add ¼″ seam
allowance when
cutting fabric

PIGGY LAUNDRY BAG
hoof

place on fold

join to leg

bottom of ear

PIGGY LAUNDRY BAG
cheek

join to body

PIGGY LAUNDRY BAG
ear

place on fold

center front

place ear between dots

PIGGY LAUNDRY BAG
upper head section

(refer to Figure 1)

appliqué
cheek
here

join to nose

butt to lower head section on dots

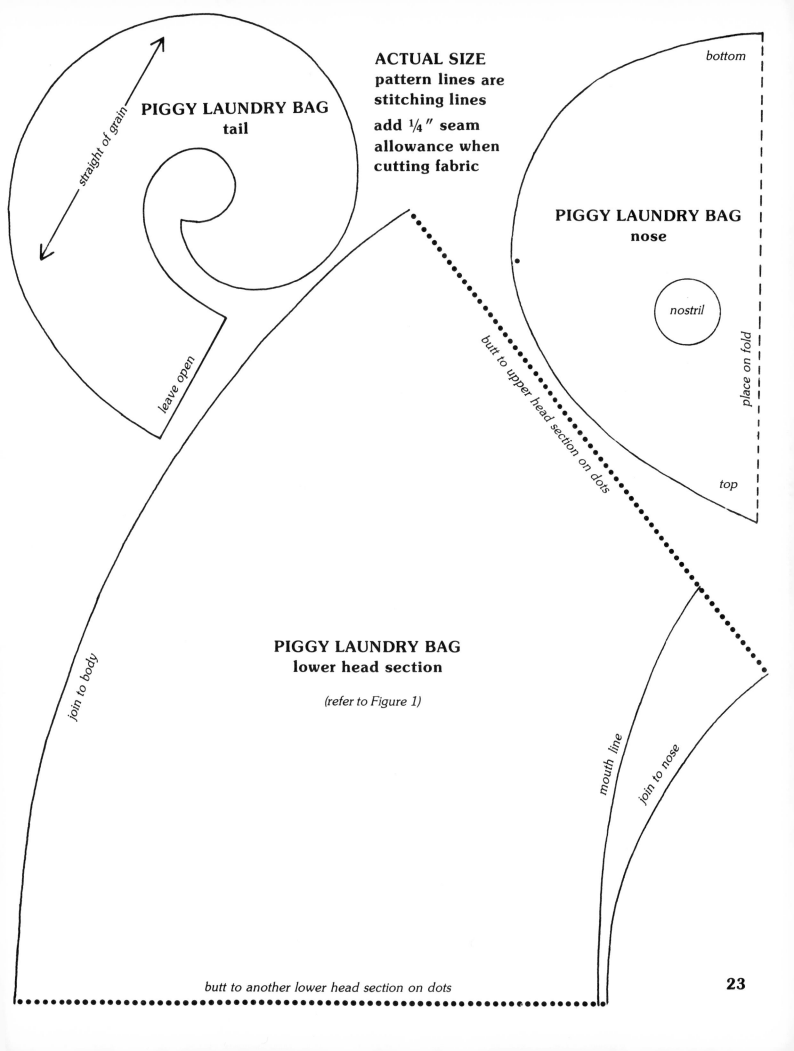

PIGGY LAUNDRY BAG
tail

straight of grain

leave open

ACTUAL SIZE
pattern lines are
stitching lines

add ¼″ seam
allowance when
cutting fabric

bottom

PIGGY LAUNDRY BAG
nose

nostril

place on fold

top

butt to upper head section on dots

join to body

PIGGY LAUNDRY BAG
lower head section

(refer to Figure 1)

mouth line

join to nose

butt to another lower head section on dots

23

(color photo, page 7)

This toddler's outfit is just as cool and crisp as a frosty slice of watermelon! You can adapt a commercial pattern to make the sundress, then use my patterns for the pockets and hat.

If you want to add green trim to the armholes, cut the dress facings specified by your pattern, but trim off the armhole seam allowance on both dress and facings. Baste the facings in place, and bind each armhole with wide bias tape. Extend both ends of the tape about 15" to tie at the shoulders. Knot the tape ends as a finish.

Two packages of bias tape (6 yards) should be enough to trim the hat, pockets, armholes and dress hem.

Watermelon Hat and Pockets

Materials

White piqué scrap, 9x25"; white thread
Brilliant pink scrap, 9x37"; pink thread
1½ yards white medium rickrack
2 yards bright green wide bias tape (for hat and pockets only); green thread
1 skein black embroidery thread

Directions

1. Trace actual-size hat pattern onto tracing paper. Trace pocket pattern onto folded tracing paper. Cut out patterns, and open pocket pattern.

2. Cut out the seed designs on hat pattern and on one side of pocket pattern to make templates. Seam allowance on hat is included; all other edges will be bound. *Pattern lines are cutting lines for fabric.*

3. To make hat lining, trace around hat pattern four times on wrong side of the white piqué; do not draw the seeds. Cut out fabric pieces. Pin and stitch two sections, right sides together. Then pin and stitch the two remaining sections together. Clip seams and press as flat as possible with the help of a tailor's ham, if you have one.

4. Join the two units with one continuous seam to complete the hat lining. Clip curves and press seams as flat as possible. Set lining aside.

5. On wrong side of the pink fabric, trace around hat pattern (and within seeds) four times, but don't cut fabric yet. Transfer seed placement lines to front of fabric, using one strand of black embroidery thread and tiny stitches. Use an embroidery hoop and two strands of black embroidery thread to satin-stitch seeds on front of the fabric. (See embroidery stitches in How-to Section.)

6. Cut out each hat section. Pin and stitch them together, following lining directions in Steps 3 and 4.

7. Place white lining inside pink hat, wrong sides together. Match up curved seams; pin, and baste together.

8. Press the wide bias tape in half along the length to make a folded binding about ½" wide. Position rickrack about ¼" from raw edges of the hat—so that half of the rickrack will be covered when bias is in place. Baste rickrack to hat. Then baste bias to hat, covering raw edges and overlapping lower half of the rickrack.

9. Use tiny hand stitches to sew bias edges to hat and to lining; stitches will also catch rickrack to hat.

10. Cut a 16" length of folded bias tape and close the long open edge with tiny hand stitches. Knot both cut ends. Fold tape into bow and tack at the center. Wrap threads around center; tack bow to top of hat.

11. To make pockets, position pattern on right side of the pink fabric, with center fold line running along the straight of grain. Trace around pattern (and within seeds) twice, but don't cut fabric. Use an embroidery hoop and two strands of black embroidery thread to satin-stitch seeds.

12. Cut out both pockets; fold each in half, right side out, and baste along the curved edge.

13. Cut two pieces of white rickrack, each about 10" long; baste one to each pocket, about ¼" from the raw edge. (See Step 8.) Extend rickrack about ½" beyond pocket at both ends.

14. Cut two strips of folded bias tape, each 11½" long. Baste bias to pocket curves, covering raw edges and overlapping

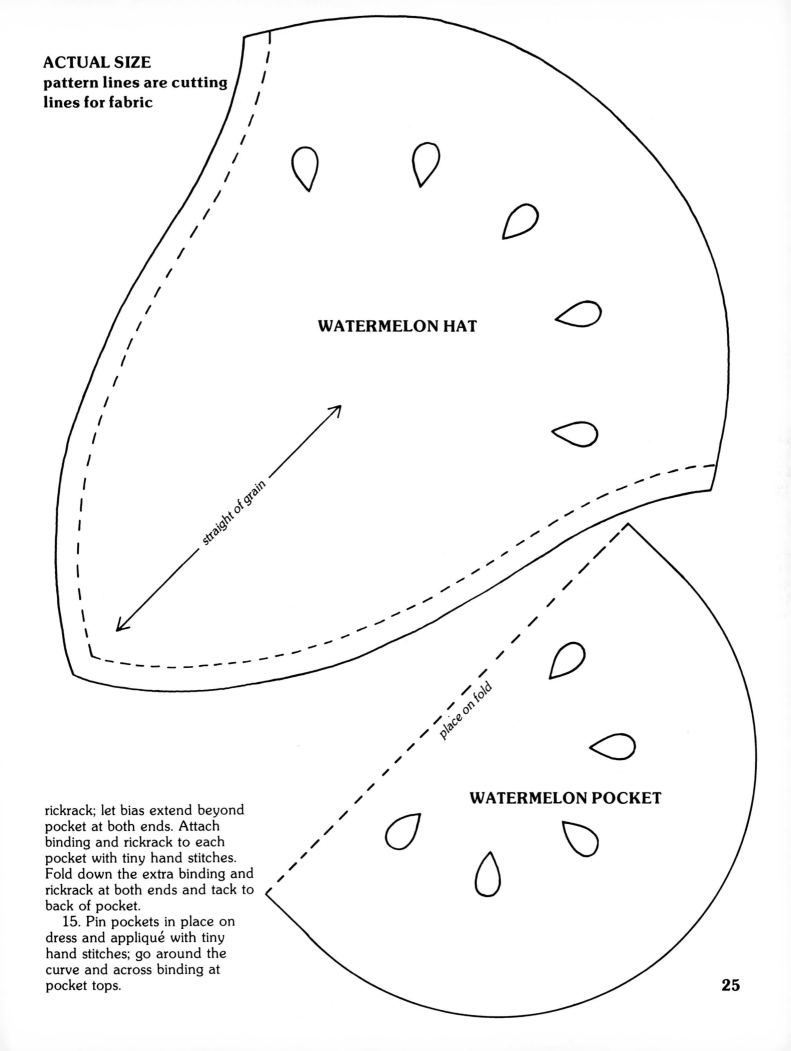

ACTUAL SIZE
pattern lines are cutting lines for fabric

WATERMELON HAT

straight of grain

place on fold

WATERMELON POCKET

rickrack; let bias extend beyond pocket at both ends. Attach binding and rickrack to each pocket with tiny hand stitches. Fold down the extra binding and rickrack at both ends and tack to back of pocket.

15. Pin pockets in place on dress and appliqué with tiny hand stitches; go around the curve and across binding at pocket tops.

For this project, use a purchased "grass green" rug. Buy an inexpensive one made of bathroom-type carpeting that can be scissor-trimmed. No exact road pattern is given since most of these rugs are not cut accurately. (Mine measured 22⅞x36¼" instead of the 24x36" that was indicated on the package label.)

The roads are made of two layers of black fabric, with a layer of quilt batting inside. After the roads are assembled, they are topstitched along the edges, and white twill tape stripes are added. The completed roadway is hand-stitched to the rug.

When I made this rug for my daughter, I found that her 1½"-wide toy trucks were just the right size for it. You could make a larger rug (or even use the design for a quilt), adding side streets, cloverleaf roads, ponds and parking lots, if you wish.

Road Rug

(color photo, page 6)

Materials

Green bath rug with trim-to-fit latex back (¾" pile), 24x36"
1¾ yards black fabric (medium weight), 45" wide; black thread
Polyester quilt batting (thin), 31x44"
5½ yards white twill tape, ¼" wide; white thread
½ yard black single-fold bias tape, ½" wide
Black heavy-duty thread

Directions

Finished size of road rug is about 32x44".

1. Custom-make your pattern by first measuring and trimming rug's sides and corner curves so they are even and accurate. Measure length and width of rug and use these dimensions to draw a rectangle in the center of a sheet of tracing paper. Place rug on paper and check for accuracy; make any needed corrections. Draw corner curves with a compass or by tracing rug.

2. Remove rug and add 4" all around the outline to create a road border. Draw center guidelines for twill tape stripes. Cut out around pattern, and fold it in quarters. Use these folds as guidelines to draw 4"-wide crossroads with center stripes (see Figure 1). Label the sections. On the A and B sections, copy dots (4" apart) where the C pieces will intersect.

3. Cut border pattern A away from center section, then cut in half on fold lines to make two A pieces, each approximately 22x32" (see Figure 2). Cut out center cross strip B (approximately 24" long), and two C strips (each about 16" long). Pattern lines are stitching lines; add seam allowance when cutting fabric.

4. Fold black fabric, right sides together, and pin pattern pieces in place, referring to Figure 3; allow ⅝" seam allowance. Draw around patterns with white pencil; cut out, adding ⅝" seam allowance to all edges. Transfer intersection dots to A and B pieces. Use dressmaker's carbon to transfer guidelines for twill tape to right side of fabric.

5. Remove patterns. Pin the double layers of fabric (right sides together) to quilt batting. Cut out each section; do not remove pins.

6. Stitch the stacked layers of each A shape together; leave seams open between intersection dots and at each end. Stitch the B layers; leave seams open between intersection dots and at each end. Stitch the layers of each C piece together; leave open at both ends.

7. Trim all batting close to stitching and at openings. Trim curved seams to ¼" and clip. Turn each piece right side out and press flat. (Turn shape A by pulling each end through the center opening.) Tuck in seam allowances between dots on A and B sections; press, but don't close any openings.

8. Working on the floor, temporarily fit both A sections to outside edges of rug, using a few pins. Trim raw edges of A so they just meet. Join edges with a whipping stitch, then cover this seam on top and bottom with black single-fold bias tape. (Use one continuous strip starting on the back; baste tape in place.)

9. Fit the B section across rug center (refer to Figure 1). Tuck the seam allowance back into each open end so ends butt against the A section. Baste in place. Position the C sections. Fit the end seam allowances into intersection openings on A and B. Baste in place.

10. Remove roadway from rug and close all openings securely with invisible hand stitches. Remove all exposed bastings. Machine-topstitch close to all road edges. Hand-baste white twill tape to roads, then machine-topstitch along tape edges.

11. Pin roadway to rug. Use black heavy-duty thread to hand-stitch inner edge of road to edge of rug. Hand-stitch crossroads in place, passing needle through to back of rug.

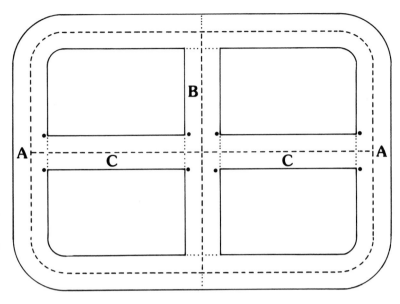

Figure 1 Roadway diagram, drawn to fit purchased rug. Broken lines show center of roads. Dotted lines show seams.

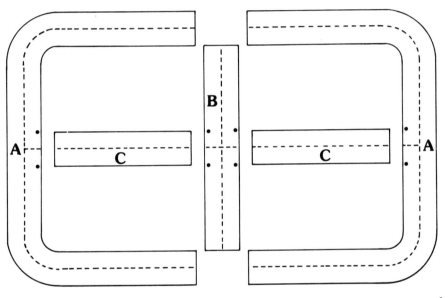

Figure 2 Roadway sections cut apart to use as patterns.

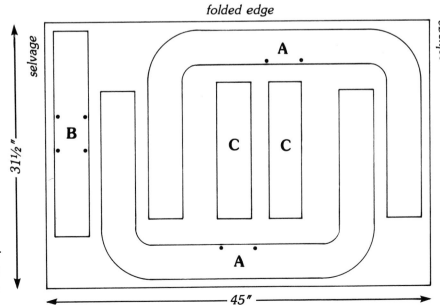

Figure 3 Pattern layout for black fabric. Add ⁵⁄₈" seam allowance when cutting.

27

Most of these designs can actually be pinned up for display, if you choose (although the cactus looks more comfortable on a flat surface).

The pincushions use up small pieces of felt and other fabric in your scrap bag. Make some ahead so you have a spur-of-the-moment hostess gift, or a head start on your holiday bazaar contributions.

Pinup Pincushions

Cactus
(color photo, page 42)

The cactus pincushion is much easier to make than it appears to be. There's a rock buried inside the polyester stuffing to keep it from tipping over. Pinking shears trim the felt edges and give it the jagged appearance so characteristic of a cactus plant.

Materials

Terra cotta felt, 5¾x11"; terra cotta thread
Green felt, 7x9"; green thread
Dark brown felt, 3½x3½"
Embroidery thread: green, terra cotta, brown
Lightweight cardboard, 2¼x2¼"
Small, heavy rock for weight
Polyester stuffing
25 straight pins
White glue

Directions

1. Trace actual-size patterns from book, copying dot marks, and cut out. *Pattern lines are cutting lines for felt.*

2. Trace pattern outlines on felt and transfer dot marks. (See transfer directions in How-to Section.) On terra cotta felt, trace one pot side, one pot rim and one pot base. On green felt, trace 12 plant sections. On brown felt, trace one soil circle.

Cut out each shape. (Cactus is trimmed later with pinking shears.) From cardboard, trace and cut out one pot base.

3. Pin two cactus sections together and machine-stitch on the inner curve, ⅛" from edge. Repeat the process to make six units. (These inner curved seams will be inside the cactus.)

4. Pin two cactus units together along the outer curve and hand-stitch together about ³⁄₁₆" from the edge, using one strand of green embroidery thread. (This seam will be on the outside of the cactus.) Use pinking shears to carefully trim seam.

Join all six units together in this way, but leave the final seam open for stuffing.

5. Securely tack the cactus units together at the top and bottom on the seam lines.

6. Stuff the cactus very firmly, using a crochet hook to pack it. Close the final seam, pushing in stuffing as you complete it. Set cactus aside.

7. Work with the pot side piece. Pin the short straight edges together and machine-stitch a ⅛" seam. Turn right side out.

8. Pin the brown soil circle to the top of the pot, matching the dots. Blanket-stitch these pieces together, using three strands of brown embroidery thread. (See

embroidery stitches in How-to Section.)

9. Invisibly attach cactus to center of soil circle, securely tacking each pinked edge of the cactus to the brown felt.

10. Stuff pot firmly, inserting rock in the middle and packing stuffing around it. (The brown soil piece will curve upward.)

11. Center cardboard base on felt base, glue together, and allow to dry. Hold base in place as you blanket-stitch it to bottom of pot, using three strands of terra cotta thread.

12. Pin together short edges of pot rim and machine-stitch a ⅛" seam. Turn right side out, fold along center fold line, and pin. Blanket-stitch raw edges together, using three strands of terra cotta thread.

13. Slip rim over base of pot, and pull it up into position. Bottom of pot rim should just cover stitching along top edge of pot, making a high collar around pot. Lightly glue rim in place.

14. Insert pins in clusters of three in all the pinked seams. Insert a cluster of seven pins at the cactus top.

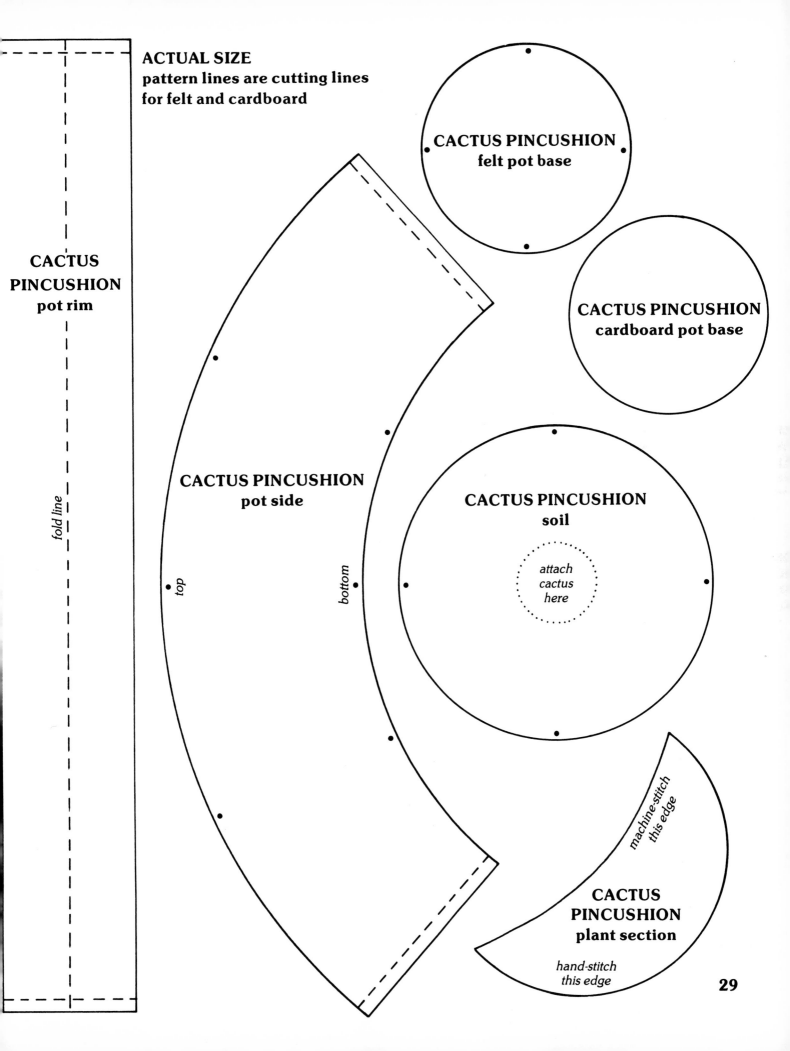

ACTUAL SIZE
pattern lines are cutting lines
for felt and cardboard

CACTUS PINCUSHION
felt pot base

CACTUS PINCUSHION
pot rim

fold line

CACTUS PINCUSHION
pot side

top

bottom

CACTUS PINCUSHION
cardboard pot base

CACTUS PINCUSHION
soil

*attach
cactus
here*

*machine-stitch
this edge*

**CACTUS
PINCUSHION**
plant section

*hand-stitch
this edge*

29

Pretzel

(color photo, page 42)

This fat pretzel pincushion studded with white "salt" pins couldn't be easier to make, and you can cut nine from a yard of 44"-wide fabric. I keep one hanging on the kitchen wall with a few threaded needles in it for dashing-out-the-door stitch-ups!

A group of fabric pretzels in a variety of golden brown prints would look nifty on a bazaar table, especially if they were placed on a checkered napkin in a large basket.

Materials

Brown with white print scrap,
4½x35"; thread to match
Polyester stuffing
Plastic curtain ring, ¾" diameter
(optional)
Pins with white plastic (or glass)
heads

Directions

1. There is no pattern for this design. Refer to Figure 1 and fold the 4½x35" print scrap in half lengthwise, right side inside.

2. Stitch a seam ¼" from the edge, curving it at start and finish; leave a 2" opening on the side for turning and stuffing. Trim and clip curved seam.

3. Turn right side out and stuff tube, flattening it as you stuff. Close opening with invisible hand stitches.

4. Twist tube into a pretzel form (see photo), and tack securely under the two rounded ends.

5. Attach a curtain ring to the back of pincushion if you wish to hang it. Add pins with white heads.

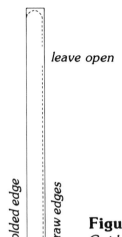

leave open

folded edge

raw edges

Figure 1
Guide for stitching Pretzel Pincushion.

Safety Pin

(color photo, page 42)

I first made this jumbo safety pin as a sachet/pincushion to include with a very practical gift of diapers for a baby shower. I sprinkled baby powder in with the stuffing, tied the felt shape with a gingham bow, and added a few diaper pins.

As an all-purpose pincushion and easy-to-make bazaar item, the design would work equally well made up in bright paint-box colors instead of pastels. To save time, you could substitute machine or running stitches for the blanket stitching. You also might want to work it up in subtle "safety pin grey" with a bright bow; then add straight pins with brightly colored heads.

Materials

Light pink felt, 5x9"
White felt, 6x9"
Medium pink embroidery thread
Polyester stuffing
⅝ yard blue gingham ribbon,
⅜" wide
Plastic curtain ring, ¾" diameter
Colored diaper pins
White glue (optional)

Directions

1. Trace actual-size patterns for spring and head sections and cut out. *Pattern lines are cutting lines for felt.*

2. Fold and pin pink felt in half so it measures 4½x5". Pin head pattern to felt and trace around outline. Mark dots for openings. Remove pattern and cut out both layers together.

3. Fold and pin white felt in half so it measures 4½x6". Pin spring pattern to felt and trace around outline. Mark overlap and dots. Remove pattern and cut out both layers together.

4. Overlap and glue or baste head to spring section on both front and back pieces. (Let the glue dry.)

5. Blanket-stitch overlap areas, using three strands of pink embroidery thread. (See embroidery stitches in How-to Section.) Blanket-stitch curved design lines on lower part of spring.

6. Pin front and back together and blanket-stitch around edge, leaving area between dots open for stuffing. Stuff firmly, but keep rather flat. Close openings with blanket stitches.

7. Use doubled white sewing thread to quilt curved design lines on the spring; pass the needle completely through from front to back. Tack head section together where curves meet.

8. Tie gingham bow to top, and tack curtain ring to back of head section if you wish to hang pincushion.

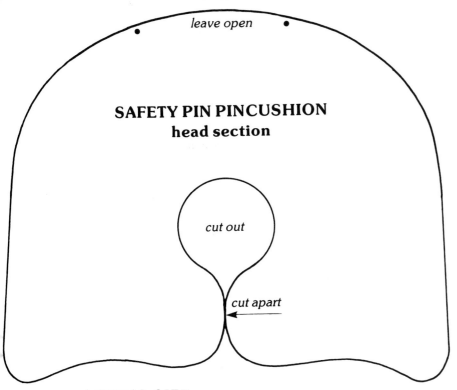

SAFETY PIN PINCUSHION
head section

leave open

cut out

cut apart ←

ACTUAL SIZE
pattern lines are cutting lines for felt

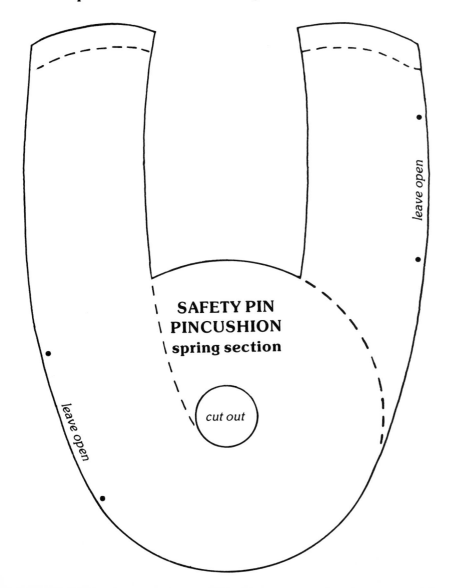

leave open

SAFETY PIN
PINCUSHION
spring section

leave open

cut out

Smiling Sun
(color photo, page 42)

One Christmas we used the sun and rainbow pincushions at the top of our tree. The rest of the tree was covered with paper, fabric, and felt ornaments, and that was the only year nothing was broken!

Materials

Deep orange felt, 6½x13"
Medium orange felt, 6½x6½"
Deep yellow felt, 6½x6½"
Medium yellow felt, 3x3"
Embroidery thread: medium orange, deep yellow, medium yellow, deep pink, black
Polyester stuffing
Plastic curtain ring, ¾" diameter
12 pins with yellow plastic (or glass) heads
White glue (optional)

Directions

1. Trace and cut out separate patterns for sun center, sunray and aureola. *Pattern lines are cutting lines for felt.*
2. Trace pattern outlines on felt. Cut out two deep orange aureolas for sun front and back. Use sunray pattern to cut one medium orange piece and one deep yellow piece. Cut one medium yellow sun center.
3. Pin or lightly glue sun center to deep yellow sunray piece. (Let glue dry.)
4. Satin-stitch the black eyes and pink cheeks, using two strands of embroidery thread. (See embroidery stitches in How-

to Section.) For each eyebrow, take a single straight stitch, using one strand of black thread. Use backstitches to embroider mouth with two strands of pink.

5. Pin or glue embroidered unit to medium orange sunray piece. Then attach to a deep

orange aureola piece.

6. Blanket-stitch all edges, using three strands of matching thread.

7. Pin front and back pieces together. Blanket-stitch together

with three strands of medium yellow embroidery thread, leaving about 1½" open for stuffing. Stuff firmly but flatly and close opening.

8. Tack curtain ring to back near the top. Insert yellow-headed pins between sunrays.

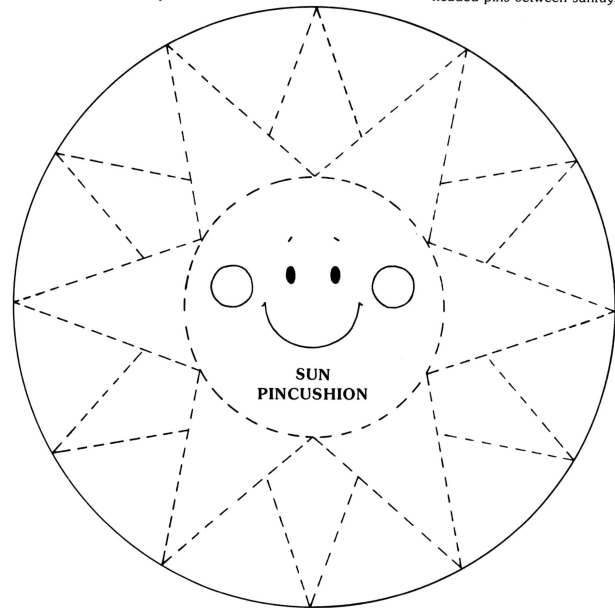

SUN PINCUSHION

broken lines show position of sunrays and center

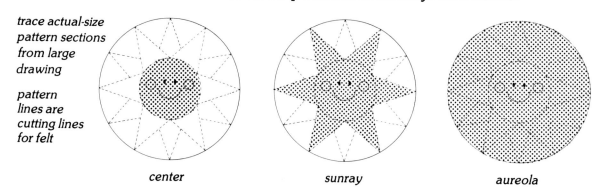

trace actual-size pattern sections from large drawing

pattern lines are cutting lines for felt

center *sunray* *aureola*

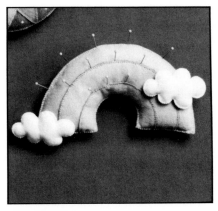

Rainbow
(color photo, page 42)

The rainbow is a sign of hope and promise. Why not hang a rainbow pincushion on the wall to remind you? Copy it in pastels or make it in bright primary colors.

Materials

Aqua felt, 8½x10"
Golden yellow felt, 3x4½"
Bright pink felt, 4x6½"
White felt, 2¼x7"
Embroidery thread: deep aqua, deep pink, deep yellow, white
Polyester stuffing
Plastic curtain ring, ¾" diameter
Straight pins with plastic (or glass) heads: 5 blue, 4 pink, 3 yellow
White glue (optional)

Directions

1. Trace actual-size pattern for cloud. Trace half-pattern for rainbow on folded tracing paper to make a full pattern (include lines for arches). From the full rainbow pattern, trace a separate pattern for each arch (A, B and C). *Pattern lines are cutting lines for back (full rainbow), arch A and cloud. Add underlap allowance to lower edges of arches B and C when cutting fabric, as directed in Step 2.*

2. Pin patterns to felt and trace around shapes. Trace one full rainbow pattern on aqua (for back), one A on yellow, and four clouds on white; cut these out on pattern lines. Trace one B on pink and one C on aqua; cut these out, adding ¼" to lower edges only (for underlapping).

3. Overlap, and pin or lightly glue pink B to aqua C. (Let glue dry.) Blanket-stitch pink arch, using two strands of pink thread.

4. Overlap, and pin or lightly glue yellow A to pink B. Blanket-stitch yellow arch, using two strands of yellow thread.

5. Pin completed front to aqua back, and blanket-stitch upper and lower arches, using thread to match felt colors. Leave the two straight edges open for stuffing.

6. Stuff firmly, but keep flat; close openings with blanket stitches, using thread to match each felt color.

7. Pin front and back of each cloud together. Use two strands of white thread to blanket-stitch the edges, leaving a small opening for stuffing. Stuff lightly and complete stitches.

8. Sew clouds to rainbow. (See photo for placement.)

9. Tack curtain ring to center back of rainbow near top. Insert pins along top of each arch.

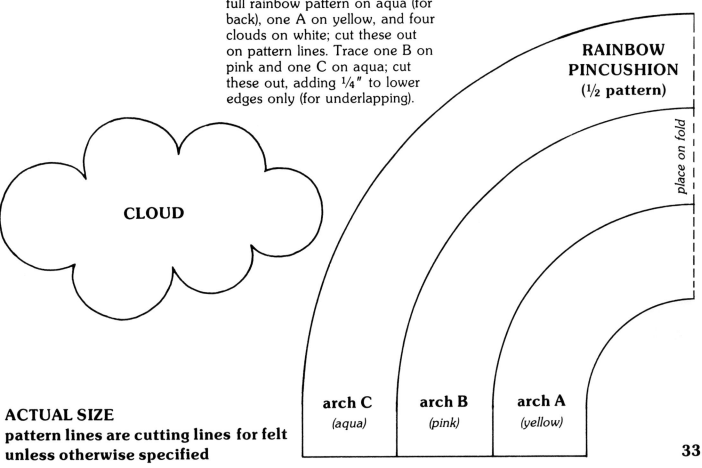

CLOUD

RAINBOW PINCUSHION (½ **pattern**)

place on fold

arch C *(aqua)*   arch B *(pink)*   arch A *(yellow)*

ACTUAL SIZE
pattern lines are cutting lines for felt unless otherwise specified

Pinwheel
(color photo, page 42)

The pinwheel is one of the quickest pincushions to make. If you're stitching many of them, save time by cutting a pattern of cardboard. You could easily enlarge this design to make a huge pinwheel pillow (without the pins, of course).

Materials

Red felt, 7x7″
Blue felt, 7x7″
Tan felt, 2x8″
White or colored thread
Polyester quilt batting (1″ thick),
   7x7″ (with thinner batting, use
   multiple layers)
Polyester stuffing
White ball button or fringe ball,
   ½″ diameter
Plastic curtain ring, ¾″ diameter
Straight pins with plastic (or glass)
   heads: 4 blue, 4 red

Directions

1. Trace actual-size pattern for blades and cut out. *Pattern line is stitching line.*
2. Center pattern on red felt and trace outline, but do not cut. Layer pieces in this order: blue felt, quilt batting, red felt (pattern side up). Place pins at close intervals all around the outside and along diagonal lines, catching all layers.
3. Use six stitches to the inch, and machine-stitch the pattern outline, making one continuous line around the complete shape.
4. Use pinking shears to cut out the square, about ⅛″ from the stitching. Make one cut into each diagonal, between the stitched lines.
5. Fold the left tip of each blade to center and tack. Adjust each blade so wrinkles are hidden within the folds and blades look smooth and puffy. Tack button or fringe ball to pinwheel center.
6. Fold tan felt lengthwise and machine-stitch ⅛″ from the long edge. Flatten resulting tube so that seam is in the middle. Stitch across one short end. Turn right side out and stuff firmly, but

Close opening and position this end about ½″ above center back of blades. Tack securely for about 1″ to give support.

7. Attach curtain ring to back of pinwheel if you wish to hang it. Insert pins around button, alternating colors.

**PINWHEEL PINCUSHION
blades**

make one cut down center after stitching

make one cut down center after stitching

make one cut down center after stitching

make one cut down center after stitching

ACTUAL SIZE

**pattern line is
stitching line**

34

Inside this plump polka dot carrot lives a bunny family of six—Mama, Papa, their little boy wearing his Super Rabbit cape, their little girl holding her favorite bunny doll, and the twins tucked in their baby buntings.

The bunnies by themselves make quick-to-stitch gifts. To save time you could substitute running stitches for the blanket stitching, make the bunnies in a variety of colored felts, and replace the clothing with narrow satin ribbon or yarn tied around the necks.

For a spring bazaar, display a bunch of bunnies in a large grass-filled and ribbon-tied basket. The smaller rabbits (baby and doll size) could be sold as springtime pins that I see youngsters wearing. Stitch a safety pin to the back of each completed bunny. Hide the bunny in a little Easter grass and tuck it into one of those colored plastic eggs that are available during the Easter season. Tie a ribbon around the egg closure and you're done!

Farmer Bunny Family in a Carrot

(color photo, page 41)

General Materials
(additional items listed under individual directions)

White felt, three 9x12″ pieces, for all bunnies
Polyester stuffing
Embroidery thread: white, black, medium pink

General Directions
Small, very sharp scissors are a must! Follow directions for each bunny, referring to General Directions as needed *(not all steps are used for all bunnies)*.

1. Copy patterns for bunnies and clothes on tracing paper, label and cut out. *Pattern lines are cutting lines for felt.*

2. From white felt, trace and cut out a front and back for the one-piece body patterns. Transfer design details to felt (see transfer directions in How-to Section).

3. Embroider face, using two strands of embroidery thread. Satin-stitch black eyes, pink cheeks and nose. Backstitch pink mouth, and use a pink running stitch to outline inner ears. (See embroidery stitches in How-to Section.)

4. Pin front to back, right sides out, and trim edges to match. Use two strands of matching embroidery thread and blanket-stitch edges together (change thread color as felt color changes). Begin with legs, gently pushing small amounts of stuffing between layers as you work; do not stuff ears.

5. For "movable" arms, head and legs, backstitch along dotted lines, using one strand of matching thread. Take stitches through both layers of felt and pull stitches tight; be sure stitches are even in both front and back.

6. Tack a fringe ball "tail" to back. (Trim fringe for smaller bunnies.)

Papa Bunny

First check list of General Materials.

Additional Materials

Red checked gingham, two bias
strips, each 1½x3¾"
Medium blue felt, 4½x5½"
Yellow and red calico scrap,
1½x1½"
Embroidery thread: medium blue,
red, yellow
1 fringe ball, ⅝" diameter

Directions

1. Follow Steps 1-3 under
General Directions.

2. To make shirt, use the two
bias gingham strips, and press
under ¼" hem allowance on all
edges. Baste one strip in place
on front arms and another on
back arms. Use two strands of
red embroidery thread to blanket-stitch shirt neck and sleeves
to bunny.

3. Trace overall patterns on
blue felt, and cut out a front, a
back and two pockets. Using two
strands of blue thread, blanket-
stitch neck, straps, armholes and
leg bottoms (on back piece); bib
top, armholes and leg bottoms
(on front piece); and both pocket
tops. Pin and blanket-stitch pockets to overalls—one to front leg,
one to back leg.

4. Add tiny running-stitch trim
to all edges of pockets and
overalls (except overall side
seams); use two strands of white
thread, and work close to the
blanket stitches. Satin-stitch yellow buttons on straps.

5. Lightly glue overall front
and back to bunny front and
back (leave straps free).

6. Join front and back sections, make "movable" arms and
head (not legs), and add tail, following Steps 4-6 under General
Directions.

7. Bring overall straps to front,
and tack in place. Fold small calico square into quarters and tuck
in back pocket.

Mama Bunny

First check list of General Materials.

Additional Materials

Floral print scrap, 2½x10"
Bright yellow and medium pink felt
scraps, each 1x1"
Embroidery thread: bright yellow,
medium pink
2" white eyelet ruffle, 1" wide
¾ yard green grosgrain ribbon, ¼" or
⅜" wide
1 fringe ball, ⅝" diameter

Directions

1. Follow Steps 1-6 under
General Directions.

2. To make dress bodice, cut
a 1¼x2½" piece from floral
scrap. Fold in half, wrong sides
together, so piece measures
1¼x1¼". Press flat, baste raw
edges together, and set aside.

3. To make skirt, fold remaining 2½x8¾" strip in half lengthwise, right sides together. Stitch
the two short ends with ¼"
seams. Clip the corners, turn
right side out, and press flat.
Mark center of long raw edge
with a dot. Machine baste ⅛"
from raw edge. Pull threads, and
gather fabric to about 3¾"; tie
threads to secure.

4. For apron, make narrow
hem on each cut end of eyelet
ruffle. Center ruffle on skirt top,
and baste.

5. For waistband, cut a 12"
piece of green grosgrain ribbon.
Mark center point. Center ribbon
on skirt top, overlapping skirt
about ⅛", and hand-stitch in
place along ribbon edge.

6. For shoulder straps, cut two
2¾" lengths of ribbon. Position
on bodice so ribbon overlaps
raw side edges of bodice about
⅛"; let ribbon extend beyond
bodice to make straps (see Figure 1). Attach with tiny hand
stitches.

7. Center top of skirt on bodice, overlapping bodice about
¼". Join pieces with tiny
stitches. At back of dress, position strap ends so they are even
with back edges of skirt; let
waistband overlap straps about
¼", and sew in place. Put dress
on bunny, adjust if necessary,
and tie bow at back.

8. Fold a 5" length of ribbon
into a bow, wrap thread around
center, and tack bow to head.

9. Cut one pink and one yellow flower from felt. Satin-stitch
a pink center on the yellow flower and a yellow center on the
pink flower. Tack flowers to
head and waist.

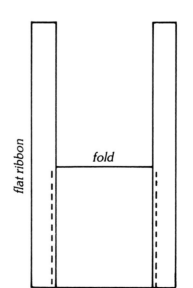

Figure 1 *Dress bodice
for Mama Bunny.*

Boy Bunny

First check list of General Materials.

Additional Materials

Medium blue felt, 2½x4½″
Bright yellow felt, 1½x1½″
Red felt, 2x3″
Embroidery thread: medium blue, red
1 fringe ball, ⅝″ diameter

Directions

1. Follow Steps 1-3 under General Directions.

2. Trace boy's suit pattern twice on blue felt to make front and back; cut out.

3. Trace shield pattern once on yellow felt. Before cutting, satin-stitch the letter R with one strand of red thread.

4. Cut out shield and lightly glue to suit front. Appliqué shield to suit by covering edges with buttonhole stitches, using one strand of red embroidery thread.

5. Lightly glue suit pieces to bunny front and back. Blanket-stitch neck, sleeve ends and pant leg bottoms, using two strands of blue thread.

6. Join front to back, following Steps 4-6 under General Directions.

7. Trace cape pattern once on red felt and cut out. Blanket-stitch all edges except neck, using two strands of red thread. Pin cape to back and join at neck with red blanket stitches.

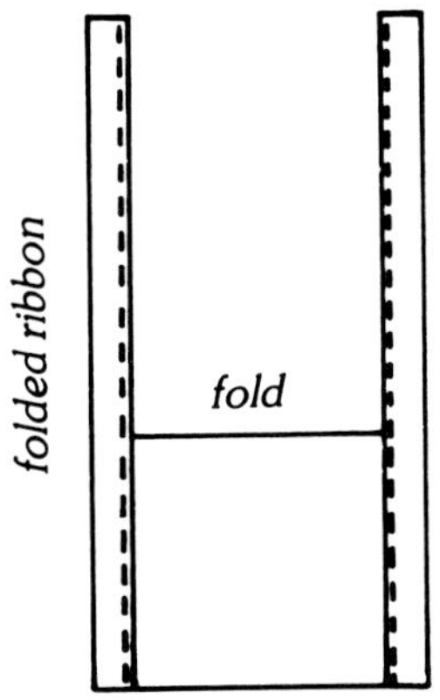

folded ribbon

fold

Girl Bunny

First check list of General Materials.

Additional Materials

Yellow and red calico scrap, 1½x7¼″
½ yard red grosgrain ribbon, ¼″ or ⅜″ wide
1 fringe ball, ⅝″ diameter

Directions

1. Follow Steps 1-6 under General Directions.

2. To make dress bodice, cut a 1x1½″ piece from calico scrap. Fold in half, wrong sides together, so piece measures 1x¾″. Press flat, baste raw edges together and set aside.

3. To make skirt, fold remaining 1½x6¼″ strip in half lengthwise, right sides together. Stitch the two short ends together with ¼″ seams. Clip corners, turn right side out, and press flat. Mark center of long raw edge with a dot. Machine-baste ⅛″ from raw edge. Pull threads and gather fabric to about 2¾″; tie threads to secure.

4. For waistband, cut a 10″ piece of red grosgrain ribbon. Mark center point, and finger-press in half lengthwise for about 2″ on each side of center. Use folded area of ribbon to bind raw edge of skirt; attach with tiny hand stitches.

5. For shoulder straps, cut two 2″ lengths of ribbon. Finger-press each piece in half length-wise and use to bind each ¾″ side of bodice; extend folded ribbon beyond bodice to make straps (see Figure 2) and join edges by hand.

Figure 2 *Dress bodice for Girl Bunny.*

6. Center top of skirt on bodice, overlapping bodice about ¼″. Join pieces with tiny hand stitches. At back of dress, attach strap ends to waistband about ¼″ from back edges of skirt; let waistband overlap straps by ¼″, and sew in place. Put dress on bunny, adjust if necessary, and tie bow at back.

7. Fold remaining 4″ of ribbon into bow, wrap thread around center, and tack bow to head.

Baby Bunny Twins

First check list of General Materials. (Use same directions for each baby, but make one pink and one aqua.)

Additional Materials

Medium pink felt, 1½x3″
Aqua blue felt, 1½x3″
Pink checked gingham, 3½x6½″
Aqua checked gingham, 3½x6½″
Embroidery thread: medium pink, aqua
½ yard narrow white satin ribbon

Directions

1. Trace bunny patterns on tracing paper, label and cut out.

2. On white felt, trace head pattern twice to make front and back. Trace hand pattern four times. Transfer design details to felt, and cut out pieces. (See transfer directions in How-to Section.)

3. To embroider face, use one strand of thread. Make black straight stitches for eyes, pink satin stitches for cheeks, pink straight stitches for mouth and nose, and pink running stitches for inner ears.

4. Trace body pattern twice on pink (aqua) felt to make front and back, and cut out.

5. Lightly glue head and hand pieces in place behind body pieces, and let dry.

6. On body front, using two strands of white thread, embroi-der four French knots for but-

tons. On body back, embroider a white satin-stitch tail, about ¼″ diameter. Finish edges of neck and sleeves with blanket stitches in pink (aqua).

7. Join front and back units, and make "movable" parts, following Steps 4-5 under General Directions, but use only one strand of thread for stitches.

8. To make bunting, fold pink (aqua) gingham piece in half, right sides together, so piece measures 3¼x3½″. Machine-stitch along raw edges, making ¼″ seams and leaving a 1″ opening. Trim off corners, and turn bunting right side out. Press flat and close opening with invisible hand stitches. Blanket-stitch around edges, using two strands of pink (aqua) embroidery thread.

9. Place bunny diagonally on bunting (ears will extend outside about ⅛″). To shape bunting (see Figure 3), fold corner C to meet bunny's chin. Bring sides to center, and tack to hold. Fold down corners B and D. Fold corner C back out of sight and tack, if you wish. Don't stitch bunny to blanket—it should be removable.

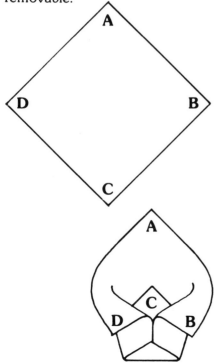

Figure 3 *Diagram for folding baby bunting.*

38

Doll Bunny

First check list of General Materials.

Directions

1. Follow Steps 1-2 under General Directions.

2. On head, using two strands embroidery thread, embroider black French knots for eyes. Using one strand of thread, embroider pink satin stitches for cheeks, pink backstitches for mouth and pink running stitches for ears. On back, satin-stitch a white tail, about ⅛″ diameter.

3. Follow Step 4 under General Directions to finish doll bunny, but use only one strand of embroidery thread.

4. Attach doll to Girl Bunny's hand with a few stitches.

Carrot

Materials

½ yard orange dot (or solid) fabric; orange thread
7″ orange zipper
Polyester quilt batting, 14x20″
2 yards green grosgrain ribbon, ⅝″ wide

Directions

1. Copy carrot pattern on tracing paper, adding dots for zipper placement. Cut out. *Pattern line is stitching line for fabric; add seam allowance when cutting fabric.*

2. To make carrot outer shell, trace pattern on wrong side of fabric four times (1″ apart), turning pattern from top to bottom to conserve fabric. Mark zipper placement dots on one section, and cut out sections with ½″ seam allowance.

3. Take section with zipper placement dot. Pin the marked edge to another section, right sides together. (This will be the carrot front.) Machine-stitch seam from each end to dot mark, then machine-baste between the dots. Trim ends of seam (but not between dots) to ¼″. Clip curves, and press seam open.

4. Hand-stitch zipper in place between dots. Remove machine basting and open zipper.

5. Join the two remaining sections, right sides together. Trim seam to ¼″. Clip curves, and press seam open.

6. Join carrot front (with zipper) to back, right sides together; make one continuous seam. Reinforce tip with second row of stitches. Clip curves, and press seam open. Trim seam, especially any excess fabric at tip.

7. To make lining, trace pattern on wrong side of remaining fabric four times (½″ apart), turning pattern from top to bottom to conserve fabric. Mark zipper placement dots on one section. Cut out sections with ¼″ seam allowance.

8. Pin wrong side of each lining section to polyester quilt batting, baste ⅛″ from edges, and cut out.

9. Take lining section with zipper placement dots. Stitch the marked edge to another lining section, right sides together, leaving seam open between dots. Join the two remaining lining sections, right sides together. Clip curves, and press the two seams open. Now join the two lining units, right sides together, with one continuous seam. Clip curves, trim tip well, and press seam open.

10. Leave lining wrong side out and place inside outer shell, matching zipper openings. Turn under zipper seam allowance on lining and hand-stitch to zipper tape.

11. To make ribbon loops, cut six strips of green grosgrain ribbon, each 12″ long. Butt the two cut edges of each strip together to form a loop, and join edges with whipping stitches. Flatten loop so joined edges are centered on the bottom, then fasten along the edges (for about ½″) with small overcast stitches.

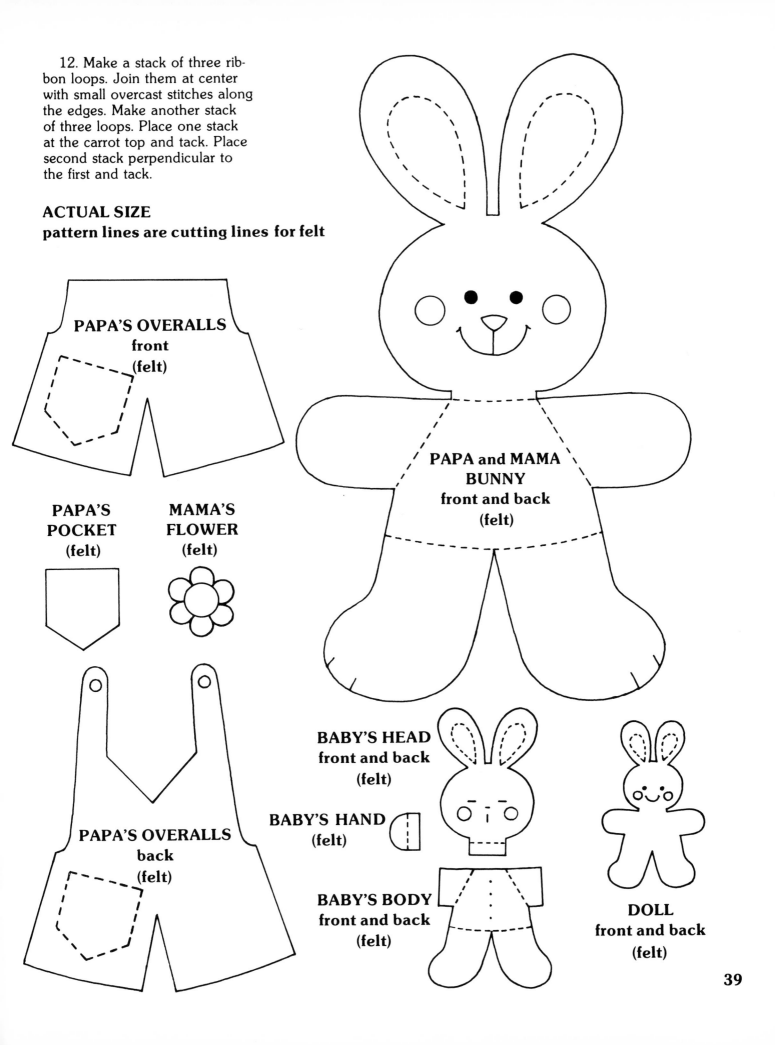

12. Make a stack of three ribbon loops. Join them at center with small overcast stitches along the edges. Make another stack of three loops. Place one stack at the carrot top and tack. Place second stack perpendicular to the first and tack.

ACTUAL SIZE
pattern lines are cutting lines for felt

PAPA'S OVERALLS
front
(felt)

PAPA'S POCKET
(felt)

MAMA'S FLOWER
(felt)

PAPA'S OVERALLS
back
(felt)

PAPA and MAMA BUNNY
front and back
(felt)

BABY'S HEAD
front and back
(felt)

BABY'S HAND
(felt)

BABY'S BODY
front and back
(felt)

DOLL
front and back
(felt)

39

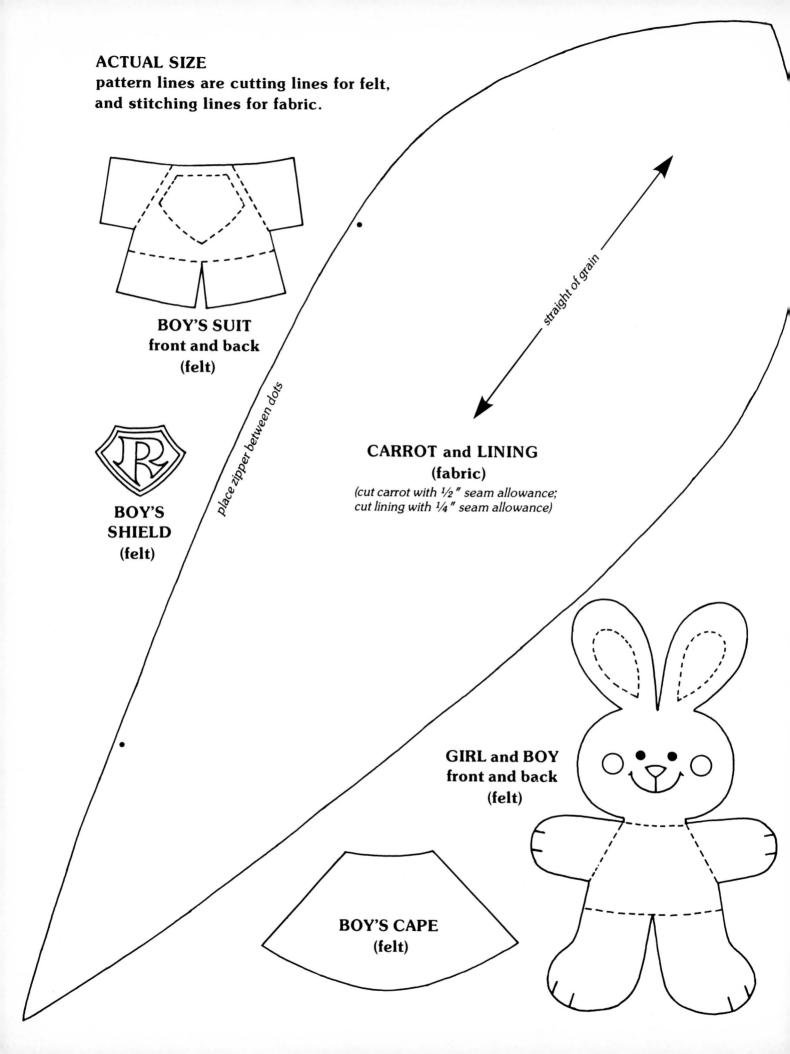

ACTUAL SIZE
pattern lines are cutting lines for felt,
and stitching lines for fabric.

BOY'S SUIT
front and back
(felt)

BOY'S
SHIELD
(felt)

place zipper between dots

CARROT and LINING
(fabric)
(cut carrot with ½″ seam allowance;
cut lining with ¼″ seam allowance)

straight of grain

GIRL and BOY
front and back
(felt)

BOY'S CAPE
(felt)

Farmer Bunny Family includes Mama, Papa, Girl Bunny, Boy Bunny, twins in buntings, and a tiny doll bunny. They all live together in the plump zippered carrot (see page 35).

Take your pick of Pinup Pincushions. Above, there's a giant safety pin, a smiling sun and a rainbow, complete with its own clouds. At right, you'll recognize a fat pretzel, a small cactus plant and a pinwheel (see page 28).

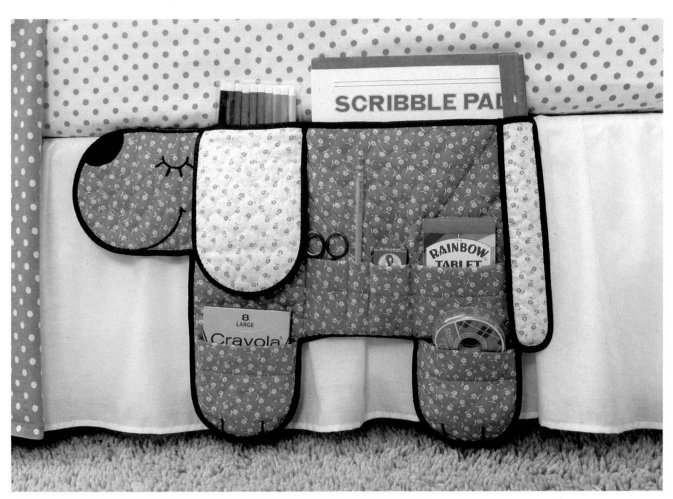

Saturday Morning Sackhound, above, holds art supplies to encourage a youngster to stay in bed—while you catch a few more winks. Nice for a child who's in bed with a cold, too (see page 54).

Cradle Diaper Bag, left, unzips to let the lid fold back. On top, there's a little bed, so Teddy Toy can slip under the covers for traveling (see page 59).

The idea for this design came about when I gave my toddler her first box of fat crayons. I was thrilled to see her delight in scribbling—on paper, the refrigerator, her highchair and the floor! The crayons seemed to come to life in her hands, so I decided to make a fabric "box" of soft crayon friends.

Her enthusiasm for scribbling coincided with an interest in putting things into containers, removing them, and putting them back again. That's exactly what she could do with this large fabric toy. The crayons and bag are my interpretation of Binney & Smith's famous Crayola ® prod-ucts, and are used with their kind permission.

If you're someone who likes "silly stuff" as much as I do, you might make up just the "box" as a tote bag for yourself.

A speedier version of the bag can be made by substituting small running stitches for the blanket stitches.

Crayon Friends

Crayons

Materials
(for all five crayons)

Felt pieces, 9x12″ each: purple, bright pink, bright green, aqua-blue, red-orange

Black felt, 4½x10″

Embroidery thread to match felt colors

Fabric scraps, 6½x8½″ each: light orange, light pink, light purple, light green, light aqua

Thread to match fabric colors

2 ³/₈ yards black jumbo rickrack; black thread

Lightweight cardboard

Iron-on interfacing (optional, but desirable)

Polyester stuffing

White glue

Directions
(same for each crayon)

1. Trace actual-size pattern pieces onto tracing paper; use folded paper for both felt tube and fabric wrapper. Cut out the patterns. Seam allowance is included when necessary. *Pattern lines are cutting lines for fabric and felt.*

2. If you use iron-on interfacing, attach it to one side of a 9x12″ felt piece. Trace patterns for felt tube, point, tip and base onto wrong (interfacing) side of felt with ball-point pen, and cut out all felt pieces.

3. Make a template of felt tube pattern by cutting out eyes, cheeks and mouth line. Use this to transfer face to right side of felt tube (see transfer directions in How-to Section).

4. Trace and cut out cardboard pieces for base and tip.

5. Embroider face, using two strands of embroidery thread. (See How-to Section for stitches.) Make black satin-stitched eyes, pink satin-stitched cheeks and pink chain-stitched mouth (substituting red-orange thread for pink on the pink crayon).

6. Pin and machine-stitch center back seams of both tube and point sections. Lightly press seams as flat as possible. Turn each section right side out and stuff firmly.

7. Use white glue (sparingly) to attach cardboard base to felt base, and let dry. Then lightly glue felt edges of base to bottom edge of crayon tube; hold until dry. Blanket-stitch edges together, using six strands of embroidery thread to match the felt color. Push stuffing toward base and add more if necessary.

8. Lightly glue cardboard tip to felt tip, and let dry. Then lightly glue felt edges of tip to top edge of crayon point; hold until dry. Blanket-stitch edges together, using six strands of matching thread. Push stuffing toward tip and add more if necessary.

9. Lightly glue edges of point section to top edge of tube section. When dry, blanket-stitch edges together, using six strands of matching thread. Set aside.

10. Trace color name onto tracing paper and transfer it to black felt, using white dressmaker's carbon and a ball-point pen as a tool. Punch-dot the letter outlines onto the felt, and embroider before cutting out the oval. Chain-stitch the letters, using two strands of crayon-colored embroidery thread. Cut out oval and set aside.

11. On wrapper pattern, cut out the oval shape to make a template. Mark placement of oval and rickrack stitching lines on right side of wrapper fabric.

12. Turn down hem at top and bottom of wrapper, press and machine-stitch. Lightly glue oval in place; when dry, blanket-stitch around it, using two strands black embroidery thread.

13. Cut two strips of rickrack, each 8½″ long, and lightly glue in place on wrapper. When dry, machine-stitch.

14. Position wrapper around felt crayon, pulling tightly and smoothing out wrinkles. Fold under raw edge at center back and pin in place. Close edge with invisible stitches.

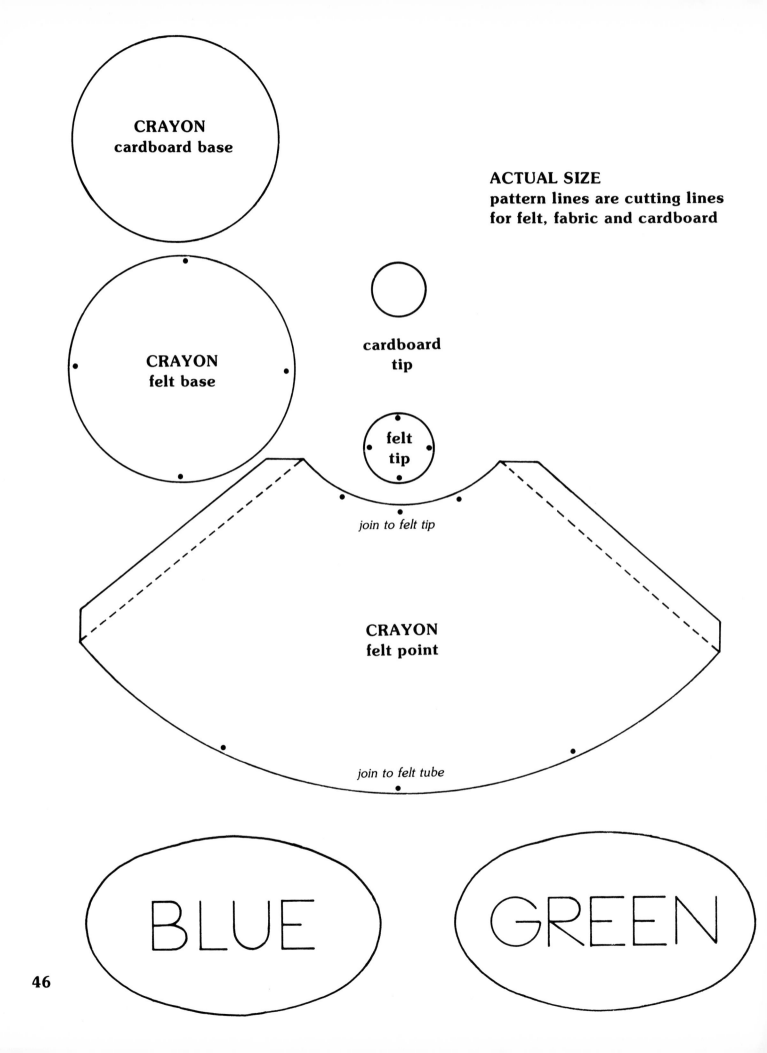

CRAYON
cardboard base

ACTUAL SIZE
pattern lines are cutting lines
for felt, fabric and cardboard

CRAYON
felt base

cardboard
tip

**felt
tip**

join to felt tip

CRAYON
felt point

join to felt tube

BLUE

GREEN

46

CRAYON
felt tube

join to felt base

guideline for wrapper placement

guideline for wrapper placement

join to felt point

place on fold

PINK

ORANGE

PURPLE

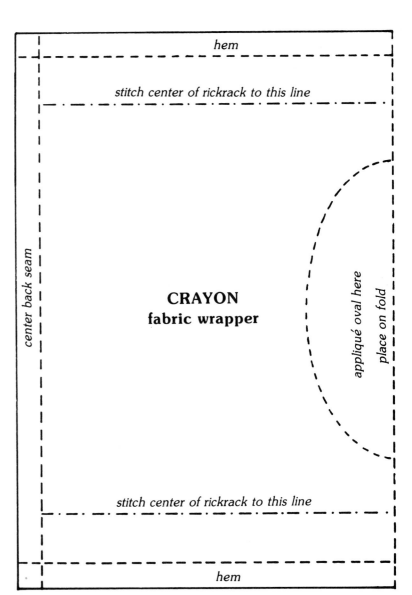

hem

stitch center of rickrack to this line

center back seam

CRAYON
fabric wrapper

appliqué oval here

place on fold

stitch center of rickrack to this line

hem

Crayon Bag

Materials

½ yard yellow-orange or gold felt, 72″ wide
Dark green felt, 14x26″ (or ¼ yard, 36″ or 72″ wide)
Light grey or beige felt, 13½x34″ (or ⅜ yard, 72″ wide)
Non-woven heavy interfacing, 18x39″
Polyester quilt batting, 18x39″
5 skeins dark green embroidery thread
Rubber cement
White glue

Directions

Press felt, if necessary, before cutting. Felt tends to shrink when pressed. Follow layouts closely; no extra yardage is allowed.

1. On tracing paper, enlarge pattern to make a bag front and a bag back, following directions in How-to Section. Position your patterns over actual-size trims A and B in the book and trace them in place. Position your bag front pattern over letters and numbers in book and trace in place.

2. On folded tracing paper, copy actual-size pattern for bag top and bottom.

3. To make the bag front flap, trace the two actual-size sections. Butt sections together along dotted lines to make one pattern piece.

4. Copy actual-size patterns for trims A, B, C and D. Make a pattern for the side/handle piece by drawing a rectangle 2⅞x50″ (see Figure 1); trace trims C and D in position.

5. Cut out all patterns. *Pattern lines are cutting lines for felt.*

6. Refer to Figure 2, layout for yellow felt. Trace and cut out one front, one back, one front flap and two side/handle pieces. Use dressmaker's carbon and a tracing wheel to transfer trim placement lines to right side of felt. Transfer letters and numbers by using a ball-point pen as a tool and punching along the out-

line. (Try not to pierce the dressmaker's carbon.)

7. Refer to Figure 3, layout for batting and interfacing. From each of these materials, cut one front, one back, one top, one bottom, one front flap and one side/handle. (Note that the side/handle must be cut in two sections and pieced. Butt and use a whipping stitch to join the two sections instead of overlapping them.)

8. Refer to Figure 4, layout for grey or beige felt lining. Cut one front, one back, one front flap, one top and one bottom.

9. From green felt, cut one top, one bottom and the following trims: two A and two A-reversed pieces (flip the A pattern over and trace the reverse side); two B and two B-reversed pieces, two C and two D pieces.

10. Trace block number and letters (5 CRAYONS) onto tracing paper. Apply a little rubber cement to the *right* side of the paper, and place tracings face down on the *wrong* side of the green felt. When dry, cut out. (Leave paper on the back if it doesn't come off easily.)

11. Glue the green letters, number and trims in place on the front, front flap, back and side/handle pieces. When dry, blanket-stitch all trim edges that will not be caught in seams; use two strands of green thread. (See embroidery stitches in How-to Section.)

12. Chain-stitch remaining letters and numbers on front flap and bag front with green thread. On front flap, use four strands of

thread. On bag front, use three strands of thread for the larger letters and numbers and two strands of thread for the smaller letters.

13. To assemble the bag, start with the bag front. Layer pieces in this order: grey felt, interfacing, batting and yellow felt (trim side up). Pin layers together and baste. (It's easiest to do this in two steps. Pin and baste two layers at a time, then join all layers.) Trim interfacing and batting, if necessary. Repeat procedure with back section and front flap.

14. Layer top and bottom sections in this order: grey felt, interfacing, batting and green felt. Layer side/handle pieces in this order: yellow felt, interfacing, batting and yellow felt (with trim side up).

15. Edge the curves on bag front and front flap with blanket stitches, using six strands of green thread.

16. Pin side/handle piece to bag front along both sides, with trim lines matching. Join with blanket stitches, using six strands of green thread; continue stitches along edge of handle and down other side. In the same way, join bag back to side/handle piece. For strength, use extra stitches at the points where side piece becomes the handle.

17. Add bottom piece by pinning the short edges (green side out) to lower edges of side/handle. Then pin long edges of bottom to lower edges of front and back. Blanket-stitch all edges, using six strands of green thread.

18. Add top piece by pinning one long edge (green side out) to back, and blanket-stitch, using six strands of green thread. Pin and blanket-stitch opposite top edge to front flap. (Flap piece is narrower than top. It should be ¼″ in from each end to facilitate closing bag.) Blanket-stitch remaining top edges with green thread to finish the bag.

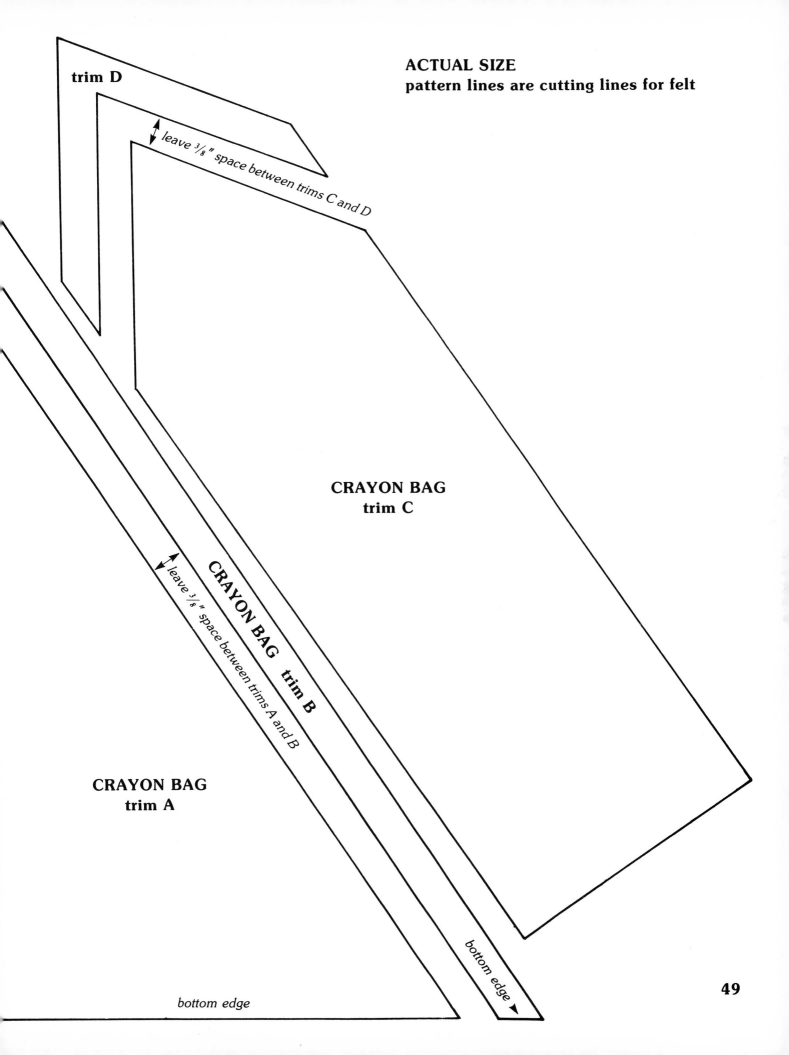

trim D

**ACTUAL SIZE
pattern lines are cutting lines for felt**

leave ⅜" space between trims C and D

**CRAYON BAG
trim C**

leave ⅜" space between trims A and B

CRAYON BAG   trim B

**CRAYON BAG
trim A**

bottom edge

bottom edge

49

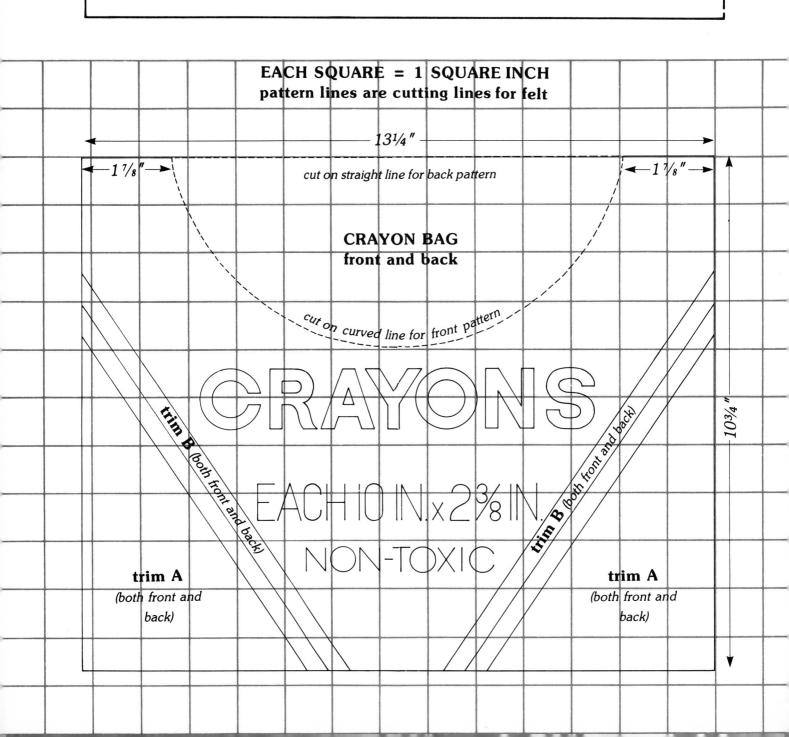

CRAYON BAG
top and bottom

place on fold

EACH SQUARE = 1 SQUARE INCH
pattern lines are cutting lines for felt

13¼″

1⅞″

cut on straight line for back pattern

CRAYON BAG
front and back

1⅞″

cut on curved line for front pattern

10¾″

CRAYONS

EACH 10 IN. x 2⅜ IN.

NON-TOXIC

trim B (both front and back)

trim B (both front and back)

trim A
(both front and back)

trim A
(both front and back)

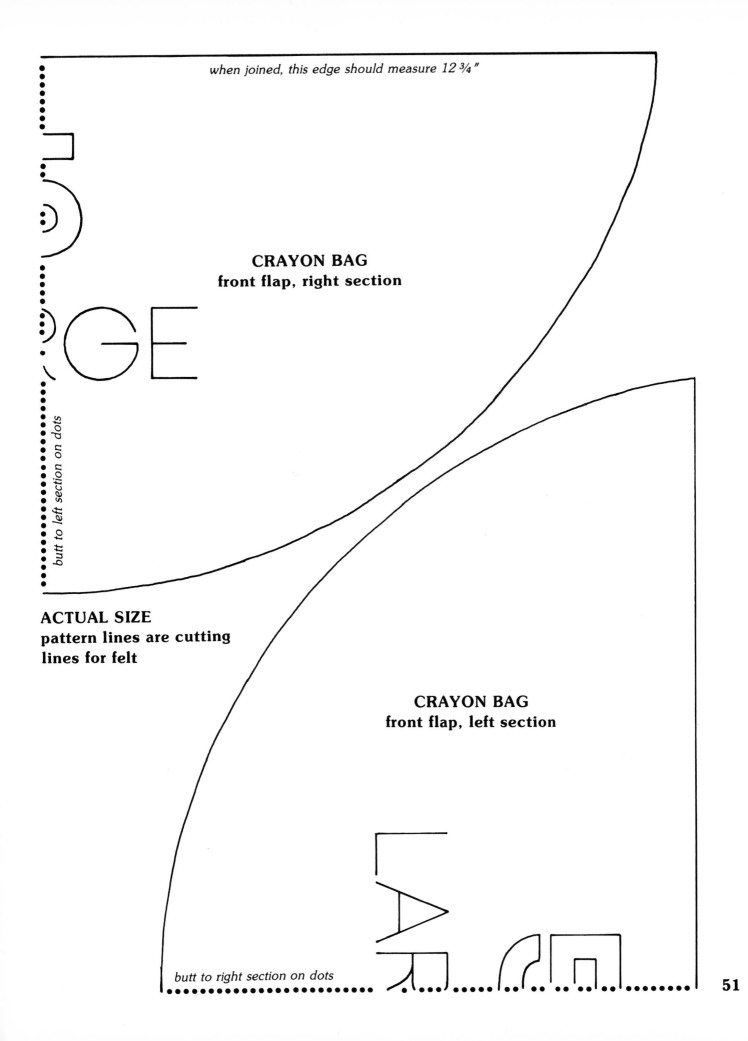

when joined, this edge should measure 12 ¾"

CRAYON BAG
front flap, right section

butt to left section on dots

ACTUAL SIZE
pattern lines are cutting
lines for felt

CRAYON BAG
front flap, left section

butt to right section on dots

when joined, this edge should measure 12 ¾"

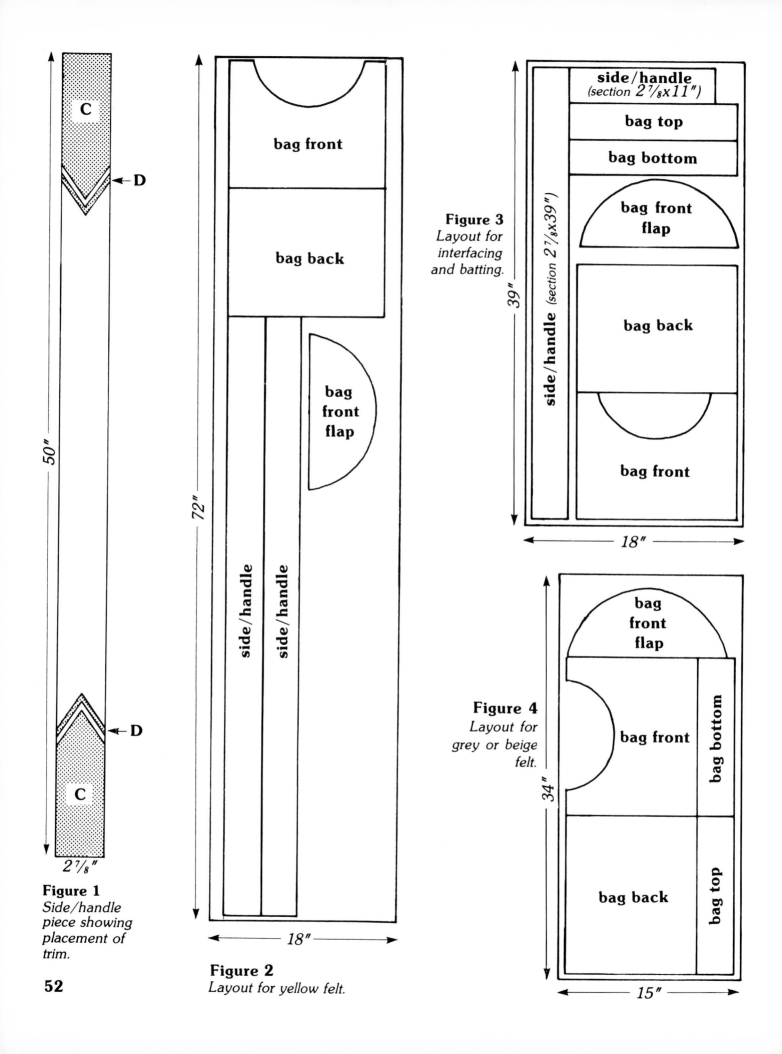

C

D

50"

D

C

2⅞"

Figure 1
*Side/handle
piece showing
placement of
trim.*

52

bag front

bag back

side/handle

side/handle

bag
front
flap

72"

18"

Figure 2
Layout for yellow felt.

side/handle *(section 2⅞x11")*

bag top

bag bottom

bag front
flap

bag back

bag front

Figure 3
*Layout for
interfacing
and batting.*

39"

side/handle *(section 2⅞x39")*

18"

bag
front
flap

bag front

bag bottom

bag back

bag top

Figure 4
*Layout for
grey or beige
felt.*

34"

15"

5

CRAYONS

EACH 10 IN. x 2⅜ IN.

NON-TOXIC

pattern lines are cutting lines for felt

The Saturday Morning Sackhound is a multi-pocketed bedside caddy made to hold a child's drawing supplies (and an early morning snack as well, if you wish). I designed it to keep our little sack artist in bed so we could sleep a little later on Saturday morning (7:30—wow!).

If you have a little friend who's about to spend some time in the hospital, this would be a fun gift, especially if you individually wrap each drawing supply.

The quilted fabric helps to keep felt pen and crayon colors from coming through to the front. However, if you'll be making this for a real free spirit, you had better line those pockets with plastic—and also include a drop cloth!

The design can be changed a bit to make a useful "wall-all" to hang over a child's desk or a baby's changing table. To do this, omit the mattress flap on the backing pattern, and enclose that top edge in bias binding before joining backing to front. Complete the dog according to directions, then sew five plastic curtain rings to the top edge of the backing for hanging.

Saturday Morning Sackhound

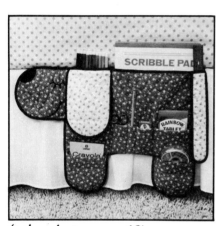

(color photo, page 43)

Materials

¾ yard quilted fabric (reversible print); thread to match
Black fabric scrap, 2x3½"
5 yards black double-fold bias tape, ¼" wide; black thread
2½ yards black embroidery thread

Directions

1. To make dog front pattern, refer to Figure 1. First, draw a 10x15¾" rectangle on tracing paper. Next, trace the face (with features and placement dot) and paws (without top hem allowance or design lines) into position. Finally, draw line *d* by extending inner line of front paw to top of body; draw line *f* by extending lower edge of head to meet line *d*.

2. To make pattern for backing with mattress flap, refer to Figure 2. Draw another 10x15¾" rectangle. This time add only the head outline. Also add a 9x18⅝" mattress flap to the top as shown in the diagram, and round the top corners if you wish.

3. To make pattern for lower leg section, see Figure 3. Draw a 5½x15¾" rectangle and mark a 1½" hem allowance inside the top edge. Trace the paws (without top hem allowance) in position. Extend paw lines to top edge to form pocket lines *a* and *d*. Mark two center lines, *b* and *c*, following measurements in Figure 3.

4. Trace separate patterns for nose, ear, tail and paw (with top hem allowance), and cut out. *Pattern lines are cutting lines for fabric.*

5. Trace around pattern pieces (face down) on wrong side of fabric. From the quilted fabric, cut one dog front, one backing with mattress flap, one lower leg section, one ear, two paws (with hem allowance) and two tails. Transfer all markings (see How-to Section).

6. From the black fabric, cut one nose. Clip and turn under the seam allowance. Pin nose in place on dog front and invisibly appliqué. Chain-stitch the eye and mouth, using six strands of black embroidery thread. (See How-to Section for embroidery stitches.)

7. To secure quilted stitching on ear, and to provide a guideline for applying bias tape, machine-stitch ¼" from edge of fabric. Pin bias tape around long, curved edge of ear, and stitch (invisible hand stitches are best).

8. Pin ear (reverse side of fabric out) to top edge of dog front (see Figure 1); have straight raw edges together. Machine-stitch top edge of dog front, ¼" from edge, catching ear in place as you go. Apply bias tape to this edge, beginning at placement dot near nose.

9. Take lower leg section and zigzag or overcast the top edge. Fold a 1½" hem to the wrong side and machine-stitch. Pin section in place on dog front and machine-stitch ¼" along outside

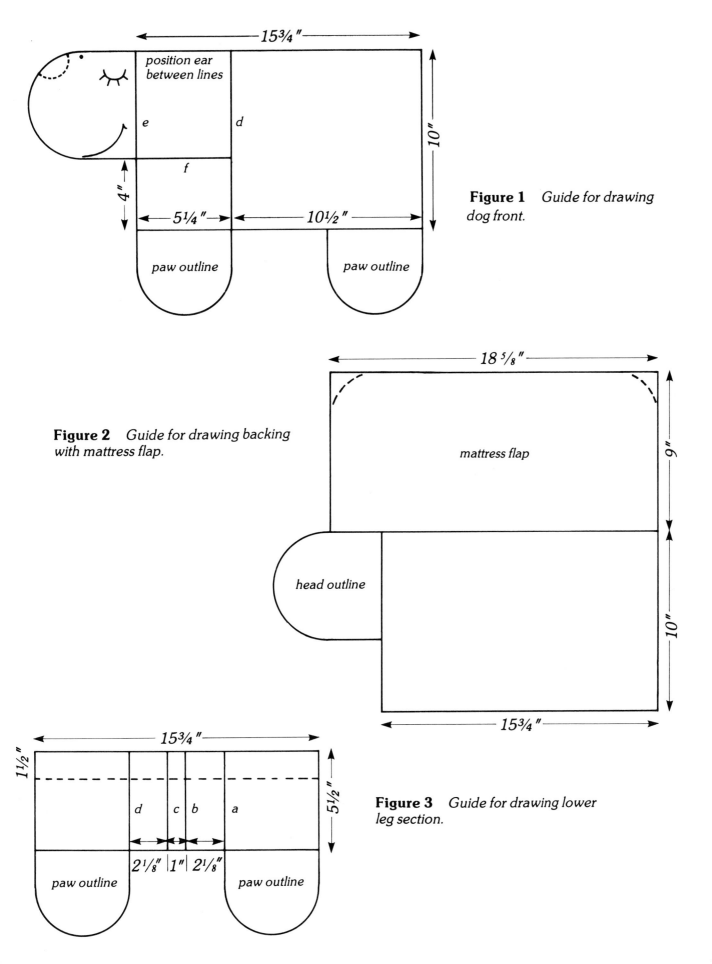

Figure 1 *Guide for drawing dog front.*

15¾″

position ear between lines

e

d

f

4″

5¼″

10½″

10″

paw outline

paw outline

Figure 2 *Guide for drawing backing with mattress flap.*

18⅝″

mattress flap

9″

head outline

10″

15¾″

1½″

15¾″

d c b a

2⅛″ 1″ 2⅛″

5½″

paw outline

paw outline

Figure 3 *Guide for drawing lower leg section.*

edge. Machine-stitch three vertical pocket lines a, b and c; do not stitch line d at front paw (see Figure 3).

10. Pin dog front with pockets to backing with mattress flap. Machine-stitch ¼" from edge around the entire dog and mattress flap.

11. Turn dog over. To finish the back, cut two strips of the double-fold bias tape, each 5¼" long. Open the center fold and press. Use the ½" flat tape to cover raw edges at top of paws; pin and hand-stitch in place.

12. Turn dog over to front side again, and fold ear up, out of the way. Machine-stitch the under-ear pocket, starting at the top of vertical line e on Figure 1. Stitch down e to f at the neck corner; turn work and stitch horizontal line f to line d. (Don't catch lower leg section in this stitching.) Complete the pockets by stitching vertical line d from top of dog front down to paw.

13. To make the paw pockets, first chain-stitch paw lines on the

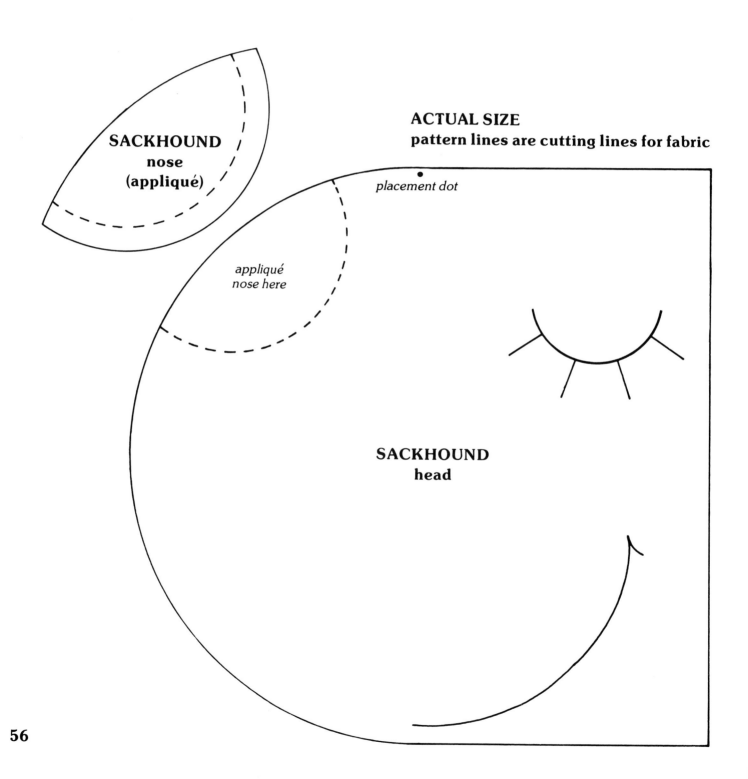

SACKHOUND
nose
(appliqué)

ACTUAL SIZE
pattern lines are cutting lines for fabric

• placement dot

appliqué
nose here

SACKHOUND
head

separate paw pieces, using six strands of embroidery thread. Then zigzag or overcast the top raw edges. Turn 1½" hems to wrong side and machine-stitch. Pin paws in place on lower leg section, and machine-stitch ¼" from outside edge.

14. Overcast or zigzag outside edge so bias tape will lie flat.

Use black bias to bind entire outer edge of dog and flap, preferably with invisible hand stitches. Close opening between nose and ear. (This is not a pocket.)

15. To make the tail pocket, use bias tape to bind the short top edge of each tail piece. Pin the two tail pieces together,

reverse sides out; machine-stitch ¼" from the edge, leaving the bound edges opened. Apply bias tape to the stitched edge, leaving ¾" extra tape at the start and finish. Turn excess tape to back of tail and tack.

16. Attach the back top edge of tail to top edge of dog front with hand stitches.

ACTUAL SIZE
pattern line is cutting line for fabric

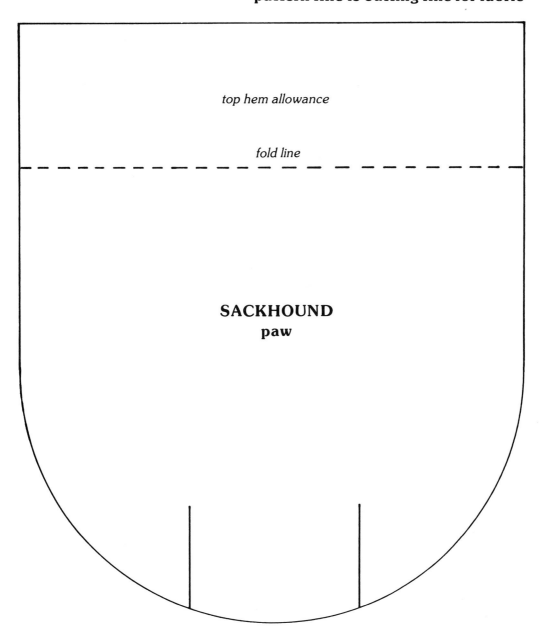

top hem allowance

fold line

SACKHOUND
paw

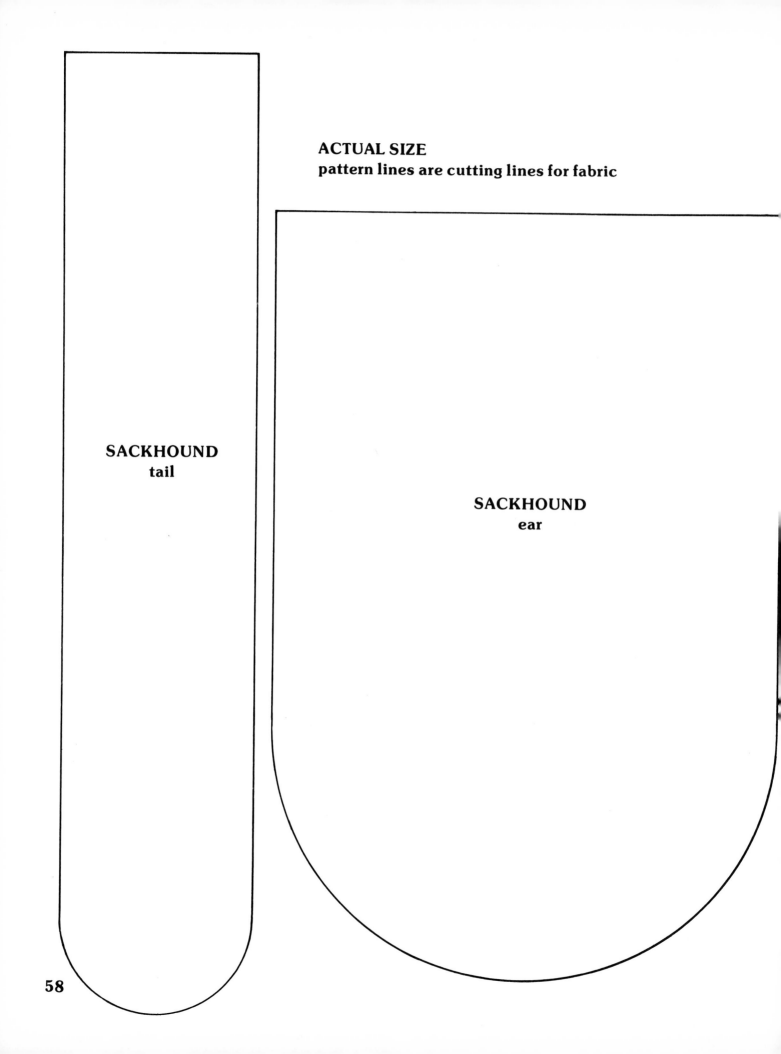

ACTUAL SIZE
pattern lines are cutting lines for fabric

SACKHOUND
tail

SACKHOUND
ear

58

I used wide-wale corduroy to make this cradle diaper bag because I wanted it to have the look of an old wicker basket.

The dusty rose "quilt" on the top of the bag is really a pocket that holds a few of Mom's supplies, as well as a soft cuddly bear for Baby. The quilted fabric is also used for lining the bag.

Twin zippers open from the center front, lifting three sides of the lid. When baby days are over, this bag might be a portable doll bed or treasure tote for Toddler.

The teddy by itself would be a sweet baby gift. Or you could make a whole collection of teddies with happy, sad, sleepy and grumpy faces to line up across the crib or hang from a mobile.

You can probably squeeze four bears from ¼ yard of 60″-wide velour, but any soft washable fabric will work well. If you do use velour, be sure the nap runs in the same direction for all pattern pieces.

Cradle Diaper Bag with Teddy Toy

(color photo, page 43)

Materials

1 ⅛ yards camel corduroy, medium- or wide-wale
1 yard dusty rose print quilted fabric
Opaque white fabric (such as piqué), 12x31″
Thread to match fabric
Polyester quilt batting (thin), 11x17″
2 camel nylon zippers, each 18″ long
7½ yards rusty brown corded piping (3 packages, 2½ yards each)
1 ⅛ yards white eyelet ruffle, 1¾″ or 2″ wide

Directions

Most seams are ¼″; only the zipper seams are ½″. You'll need a zipper foot attachment for your sewing machine to stitch the piping.

1. Trace actual-size pattern for side end A on folded tracing paper; mark center top and center bottom with dots. Don't make paper patterns for rectangles. You will draw rectangles directly on wrong side of fabric.

2. Before cutting fabric, mark all placement dots, stars and lines, and label each fabric piece with the proper letter within the seam allowance. *Pattern lines are cutting lines for fabric.*

3. To cut corduroy, determine the way you want nap to run and refer to Figure 1 for layout. On wrong side of fabric, trace two of end A pattern, and draw rectangles, following dimensions given. (See Figure 2 for more detailed drawing of front rim B piece.) Transfer all placement lines and label each piece. (See transfer directions in How-to Section.)

4. To cut quilted lining, refer to Figure 3. On wrong side of fabric, trace two of end A, and draw rectangles, following dimensions given. Transfer placement lines and label each piece. After cutting out pieces, stitch along all edges of the quilted fabric to keep the quilting stitches from unraveling.

5. To cut white fabric, refer to Figure 4. Measure and draw directly on wrong side of fabric.

6. Start by making corduroy outer shell. Check nap directions and pin the two front rim B pieces, right sides together, along the zipper seam. (Do not pin edges marked with stars.) Machine-baste ½″ seam, and press open.

7. Pin the two zippers in place, face down on the seam line, with zipper pulls meeting at center front. (Zipper tapes will overlap.) Taper ends of zipper tapes near pulls, and pin ends away from seam line. Use tiny backstitches to insert zipper by hand for neatest appearance. Remove basting.

8. Machine-stitch the rim-zipper unit to back rim C along the short edges, right sides together. Start and stop seams exactly ¼″ **59**

from the raw edges; do not stitch into seam allowances. (If metal zipper "stops" fall on the seam lines, sew seams by hand with small backstitches.)

9. Before attaching corded piping, check the piping seam allowance. It should be $\frac{1}{4}$"; trim if necessary.

10. Begin at center back of completed rim unit, and pin corded piping to one raw edge. Place piping on right side of fabric, with raw edges flush. Machine-stitch on seam line, using zipper foot attachment. Clip seam allowance to seam line at two points marked with stars.

(To join piping, open bias tape surrounding cord, trim off $\frac{1}{2}$" of cord, tuck under raw edge of tape, and let tape overlap adjoining piece of piping. Join with tiny hand stitches.) Set rim aside.

11. Stitch piping to curved edge of each end A piece, placing piping on right side of fabric. Set end pieces aside.

12. Pin side D pieces, right sides together, along one long edge; stitch a $\frac{1}{4}$" seam to make a complete side section. (Nap on adjoining corduroy pieces should run in opposite directions for the best appearance on finished bag.) Press seam open.

13. Machine-stitch both long (20$\frac{1}{2}$") edges of this side section on the seam lines; clip into the seam allowance almost to the stitching, making cuts about $\frac{1}{2}$" apart. Pin one clipped edge to the curved edge of one end A piece, right sides together. Machine-stitch, and clip seam allowance. Repeat procedure to attach the remaining curved end A piece.

14. Add corded piping to the top edge of this completed lower bag, beginning at the center of one side. Pin piping to right side of corduroy, with raw edges flush. Stitch on seam line. Set piece aside.

15. Work with one handle piece E, and stitch corded piping to right side of both long edges. Pin to another handle piece E,

right sides together, and stitch both long edges. Turn handle right side out and press flat. Repeat to make second handle.

16. Trim handle ends so they are the same length and at right angles to the long edges; close cut ends with machine stitches.

17. Pin each handle to one side of bag, with handle ends 2" from a corner seam (see photo for position). Keep raw edges of handle even with raw edges of lower bag (handle will be against side piece for sewing). Machine-stitch in place.

18. To make lid, pin wrong side of white sheet F to quilt batting, smoothing out wrinkles. Hand-baste all sides within the seam allowance. Trim batting flush with fabric, and set piece aside.

19. Fold white sheet cuff H in half lengthwise, right side out, and press. Machine-stitch the long raw edge within the seam allowance.

20. Pin stitched edge of cuff to wrong side of dusty rose quilt top G (a 10$\frac{1}{2}$" edge). Machine-stitch. Press seam open, then press cuff down onto right side of quilt top; pin in place.

21. Cut an 11" piece of eyelet ruffle, and pin in place under folded edge of cuff. (Be sure ruffle extends to side seams; trim if necessary.) Invisibly stitch edge of cuff and ruffle to quilt top.

22. To complete lid, baste quilt top to white sheet/batting F piece, matching bottom and side edges. Machine-stitch all around lid, $\frac{1}{4}$" from edge.

23. Pin completed lid to rim (piping edge), right sides together. Start with the two long edges of lid, matching clips on rim (at stars) to corners of lid. Machine-stitch long edges between clips, then pin and stitch both short edges between clips. Trim off the corners.

24. Turn lower section of bag

inside out, with handles inside. Pin this section to lower edge of rim, right sides together. Stitch one edge at a time, keeping zipper partially open for ease in turning right side out. Then put bag aside.

25. Complete quilted lining for lower bag, following directions in Step 12-13. (No piping is used in the lining.)

26. To make the lid lining, machine-stitch the starred (long) side of each rim B piece, $\frac{1}{4}$" from the edge. Clip almost to the stitched line at the stars.

Machine-stitch $\frac{1}{2}$" from edge on both remaining long edges (zipper side), and press seam allowance to back of fabric.

Pin and stitch both rim B pieces to back rim C piece, right sides together, along the short edges. (Pressed edges of rim B pieces will butt against each other.)

27. Join completed rim to inner lid F, following lid directions in Step 23. (No piping is used in lining.) Then join lower edge of rim to lower bag lining.

28. Turn lining inside out; insert in bag so printed fabric is right side out. Use pins to fit lining inside bag. Tack invisibly at lid corners (inside) and at center of lining under lid, taking care not to catch pocket in stitches.

29. To make pillow, baste eyelet ruffle around edge of one white pillow I piece, right sides together. (Scalloped edge will point toward center of pillow, and ruffle binding will run along cut edge of fabric.) Fold ruffle binding at corners so ruffle will be extra full there; pin ruffle fullness out of the way.

30. Use second I piece as the back and pin to front, right sides together. Machine-stitch around edge, leaving about 2" open for turning. Clip off corners and turn right side out. Stuff lightly and close opening with invisible hand stitches.

31. Tack pillow in place on lid top. (Bottom ruffle of pillow will be under quilt.)

Figure 1 *Layout for corduroy fabric; seam allowance is included.*

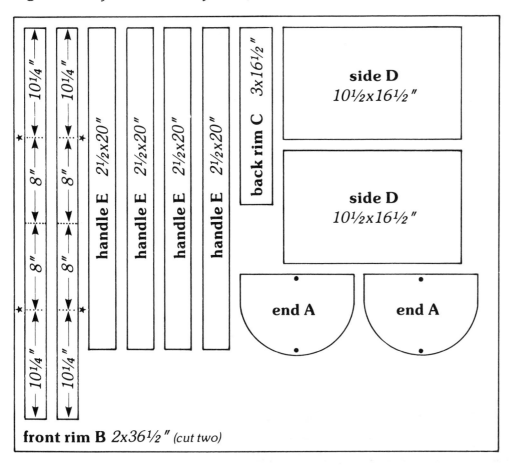

Figure 2 *Guide for drawing front rim B piece.*

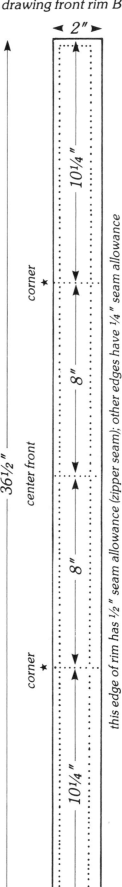

Figure 3 *Layout for quilted fabric; seam allowance is included.*

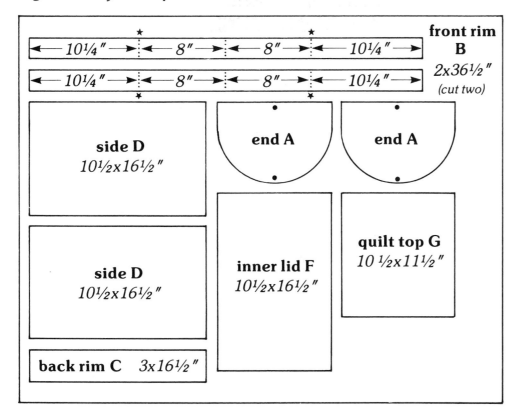

Figure 4 *Layout for white fabric; seam allowance is included.*

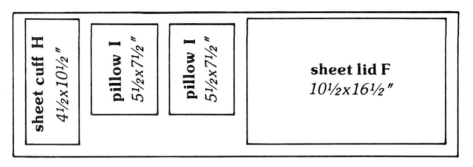

sheet cuff H
4½x10½"

pillow I
5½x7½"

pillow I
5½x7½"

sheet lid F
10½x16½"

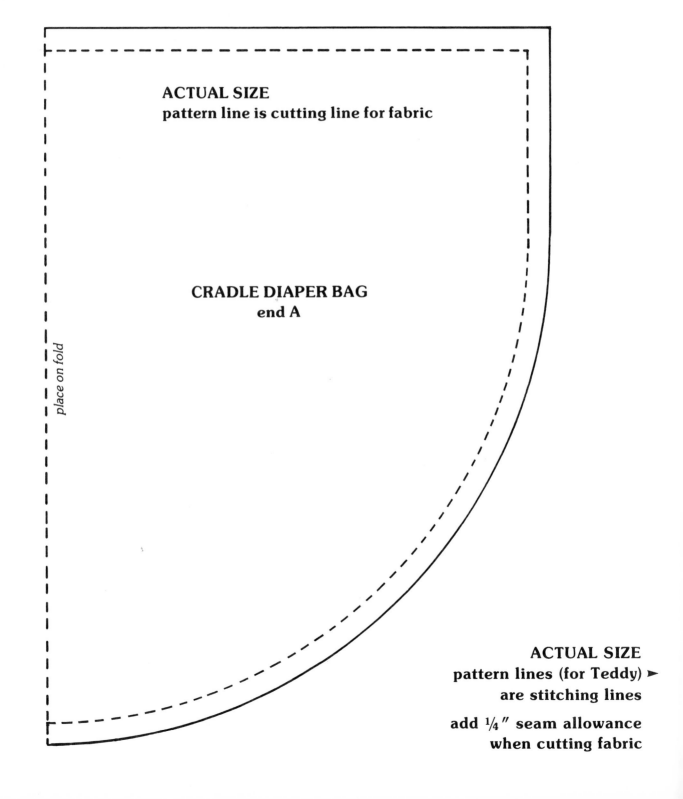

ACTUAL SIZE
pattern line is cutting line for fabric

CRADLE DIAPER BAG
end A

place on fold

ACTUAL SIZE
pattern lines (for Teddy) ►
are stitching lines

add ¼" seam allowance
when cutting fabric

Teddy

Materials

Cinnamon velour scrap (washable),
  9x17"
½ yard aqua satin ribbon, ¼" wide
Embroidery thread: 1 yard black,
  1 yard peach
Polyester stuffing

Directions

1. Trace actual-size patterns, copying all placement dots and features, and cut out. On body pattern, cut out cheeks and nose to make a template. *Pattern lines are stitching lines; add seam allowance when cutting fabric.*

2. Check direction of nap, and pin each pattern piece to wrong side of velour fabric. Trace around pattern outlines, drawing two body pieces, four ears, four arms and four legs. Transfer all body placement dots to wrong side of fabric.

3. Cut out pieces, adding ¼" seam allowance.

4. Hand-baste around entire seam allowance of the separate front and back pieces. Transfer facial features to right side of bear front (see transfer directions in How-to Section).

5. Pin body front and back, right sides together. Machine-stitch on seam lines, leaving areas open between dots on head and sides, as well as entire bottom seam. Clip V areas at neck, and trim seams along stitching (do not trim areas not stitched). Turn right side out.

6. Pin ear, arm and leg pieces, right sides together. Machine-stitch, leaving straight edges open. Clip curves (or trim with pinking shears). Turn pieces right side out.

7. Lightly stuff body, arms and legs (not ears).

8. Close open seams on legs, arms and ears with basting stitches, ¼" from the raw edge; pull stitches to fit openings on body. Insert ears and arms in proper openings. Tuck under body seam allowance at these points and close openings with invisible hand stitches, catching ears and arms in place.

9. Stuff lower body, pin legs in place, and close body seam with invisible hand stitches.

10. Embroider face, using two strands of thread to satin-stitch a black nose and mouth, and peach cheeks. (See embroidery stitches in How-to Section.) Chain-stitch black eyes. Use a straight stitch for black eyebrows.

11. Tie aqua ribbon around neck in a bow, and tack securely at bow. Tuck teddy under quilt on lid of diaper bag.

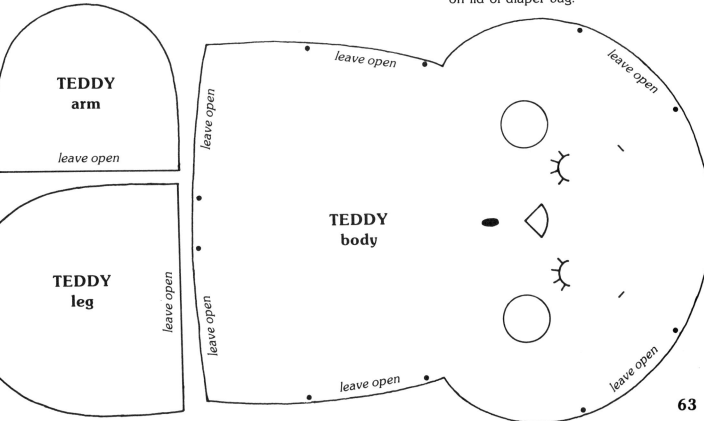

TEDDY ear — *leave open*

TEDDY arm — *leave open*

TEDDY leg

TEDDY body

leave open

63

Here's a collection of potholders that may provide ideas for little gifts or bazaar fare.

The HOT set looks best in hot colors, I think, but you might choose to work it up in colors to match a friend's kitchen.

Polka dot fabric supplies the "pepper" in the pepper shaker and the "peas" in the Mason jar. (You didn't really think I embroidered all those little dots, did you?) If you have difficulty finding color dotted fabric for peas, corn and other "canned" foods, you could substitute solid colors. In that case, you may prefer to slip in a piece of plain white fabric for the cap area of the Mason jar. Experiment and discover the look you like best.

To maintain the shapes of the salt and pepper shakers and the Mason jar, I added the bias tape by hand instead of using the sewing machine. This made the potholders good "take along" handwork.

For safety's sake, consider adding a portion of an old Teflon-coated ironing board cover to the backs of the potholders (inside or outside). In any event, make sure the batting you use is thick enough to give suitable protection.

Potholders

HOT Potholders
(color photo, page 78)

Materials (for each set)

Red fabric scrap, 7½x22½"
Orange fabric scrap, 7½x22½"
Red or orange print (or solid) fabric scrap, 7½x22½", for backs; matching thread
Thick polyester quilt batting (or multiple layers of thin batting), 7½x22½"
1 ⅜ yards white single-fold bias tape
3 yards white wide bias tape; white thread
3 plastic curtain rings, ¾" diameter (optional)

Directions

1. The letter patterns are actual size. Copy them on folded tracing paper and cut out a complete pattern for each letter. *Pattern lines are cutting lines for fabric.*

2. Trace patterns on red fabric and lightly transfer tape guidelines. (See transfer directions in How-to Section.) Cut out one of each letter; do not add seam allowances.

3. Cut three orange squares, three print or solid squares (for backs), and three quilt batting squares, each 7½x7½".

4. Baste a red letter to each of the orange squares. Position the ½"-wide bias tape so it covers the inside raw edges of the H, O and T. (Half of the tape should be on the red letter and half on the orange background.) Miter tape at corners (see How-to Section). Baste both edges of tape with invisible stitches so they can be left in the work.

5. For each potholder, layer pieces in this order: back (wrong side up); batting; front (right side up). Baste edges together, trim batting if necessary, then overcast edges to hold them for binding. Place pins within the letter to keep fabric from shifting, and machine-stitch along both edges of tape to quilt the layers.

6. If you're not using curtain rings for hangers, make a bias loop for each potholder.

Fold a 3" length of ½"-wide bias tape down the center and stitch both long edges. Form a loop and sew raw ends to the top center edge of potholder; loop stays down flat against potholder. (If you are using curtain rings, add them last; see Step 9.)

7. Fold and press all the wide bias tape so one edge is ½" wide. Pin folded tape to the outside raw edge of each potholder, with the ½" width on the front; miter tape at corners. Baste tape to front, using invisible stitches so they can be left in the work. Baste tape to back, making stitches secure since this edge may not be caught when you machine-stitch.

8. Keep pins within each letter and machine-stitch along front edge of tape. (For a neat finish on the back, use bobbin thread to match the back fabric.) Knot all the threads and use a needle to bury loose ends inside the potholders.

9. If you are using curtain rings, tack one to the top center edge of each potholder.

64

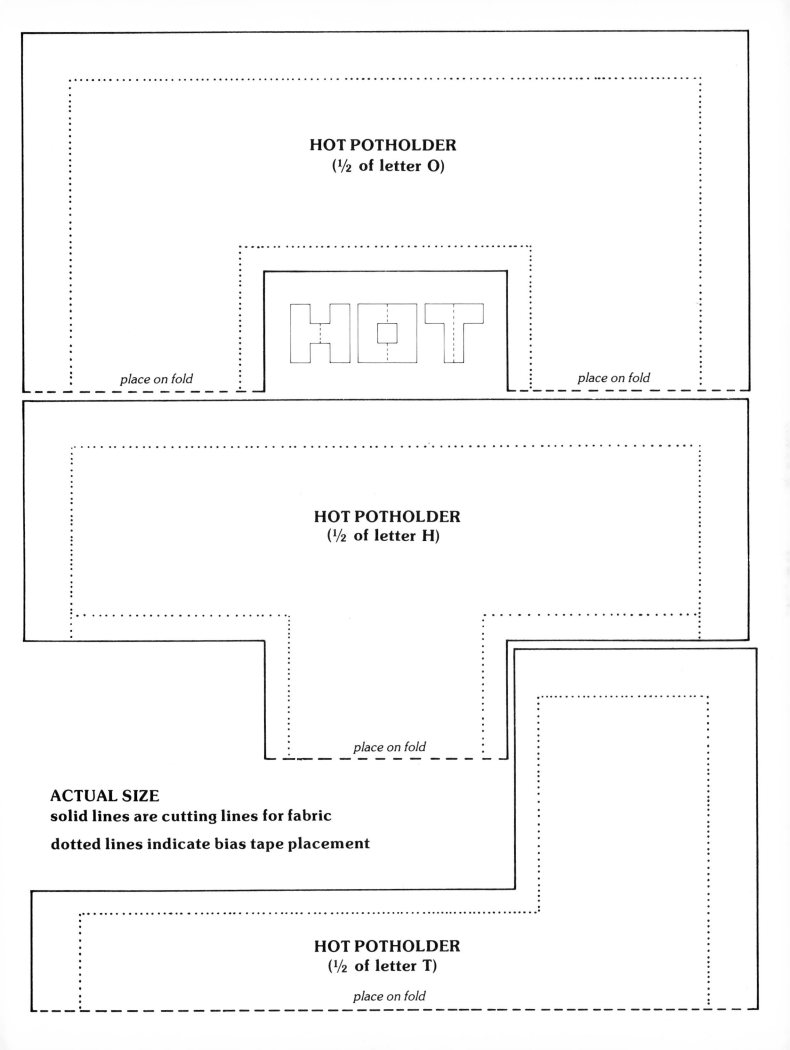

HOT POTHOLDER
(½ of letter O)

place on fold   *place on fold*

HOT

HOT POTHOLDER
(½ of letter H)

place on fold

ACTUAL SIZE
solid lines are cutting lines for fabric

dotted lines indicate bias tape placement

HOT POTHOLDER
(½ of letter T)

place on fold

Salt and Pepper Potholders

(color photo, page 78)

Materials (for each set)

White fabric scrap, 4¾x7½"
White with black dot fabric scrap, 4¾x7½"
Red fabric scrap, 12¼x15"
Thick quilt batting (or multiple layers of thin batting), 8¼x15"
3 yards black double-fold bias tape, ¼" wide; black thread
Black embroidery thread
2 plastic curtain rings, ¾" diameter (optional)

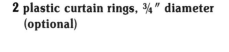
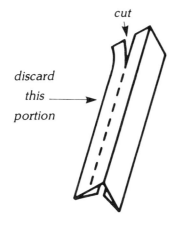

Figure 1 *Trimming double-fold bias tape to use as a ¼" flat trim.*

Directions

1. Shaker pattern is actual size. Trace and cut out the complete shape; copy only the two vertical bias placement lines on this piece.

From the same drawing, trace and cut out pattern for cap section; copy the two horizontal bias placement lines and the shaker holes. With an X-acto knife or ¼" paper punch, cut out small holes to make a template. *Pattern lines are cutting lines for fabric.*

2. Pin complete shaker pattern to fabrics and batting. Trace and cut out the following: one white piece, one dotted piece, two red pieces (for backs) and two batting pieces.

Transfer vertical bias placement lines to front of white and dotted pieces. (See transfer directions in How-to Section.)

3. Trace around cap pattern twice on red fabric, but don't cut out. Transfer shaker holes and the two horizontal bias placement lines. Before cutting, satin-stitch the five holes on each cap, using two strands of black embroidery thread. (See embroidery stitches in How-to Section.) Cut out caps and set aside.

4. Cut a piece of black double-fold bias tape 41" long. This will be used as a flat trim, ¼" wide. To remove bulk, trim one side of the tape, about ⅛" from the center fold (see Figure 1). Discard narrow portion.

From trimmed tape, cut four strips, each 4⅜" long, and four strips, each 5⅜" long.

5. Baste a 4⅜" strip of bias to both lower vertical lines on the white and the dotted shaker pieces (top of tape will be covered by cap sections). Invisibly stitch in place.

6. Baste the red cap sections in position. Baste a 5⅜" strip of trimmed bias to both horizontal lines on each cap (bottom strip covers raw edge of red cap). Invisibly stitch in place.

7. Layer the pieces for each potholder in this order: back (wrong side up); batting; front (right side up). Baste around shape about ¼" from the edge to provide a guideline for tape placement. Trim edges of batting if necessary, and overcast the edges.

8. If you are not using curtain rings for hangers, make bias tape loops, following Step 6 under the HOT Potholders.

9. Baste black double-fold bias tape to outside raw edge of each potholder. Fold tape into V areas of cap to maintain shape. Use invisible hand stitches to apply tape, first to front and then to back.

10. If you are using curtain rings, tack one to the top center edge of each potholder.

ACTUAL SIZE
pattern line is cutting line for fabric

broken lines indicate bias tape placement

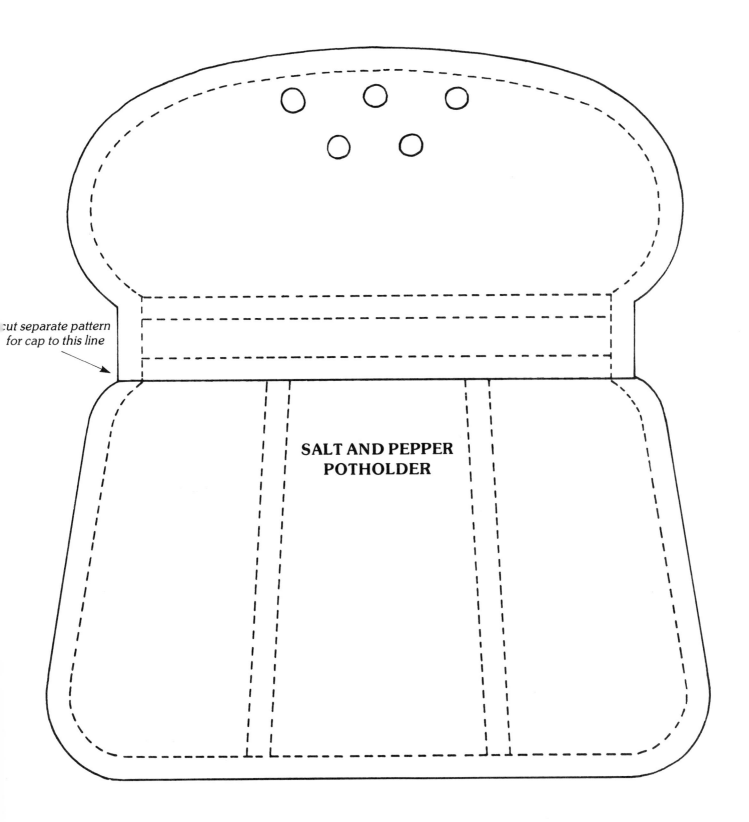

cut separate pattern
for cap to this line

**SALT AND PEPPER
POTHOLDER**

Mason Jar Potholder
(color photo, page 78)

Materials

White with green dot fabric scrap, 8½x15"

White fabric scrap, 5½x5½", for label

Thick polyester quilt batting (or several layers of thin batting), 7½x8½"

1¾ yards black double-fold bias tape, ¼" wide; black thread

18" red double-fold bias tape, ¼" wide; red thread

1 yard black embroidery thread

1 plastic curtain ring, ¾" diameter (optional)

Directions

1. Pattern for the Mason jar is actual size. Trace jar, adding placement lines for horizontal bias tapes and label, and cut out. From the same pattern, trace the label (including letters), and cut out. *Pattern lines are cutting lines for fabric.*

2. Pin the jar pattern to dotted fabric, folded right sides together. Trace pattern and cut out front and back pieces together. Transfer placement lines for bias tape and label to the jar front. (See transfer directions in How-to Section.) Trace jar pattern on batting and cut out.

3. Trace pattern for label twice on white fabric, and transfer the letters to one piece (second piece is for backing).

Before cutting out label, chain-stitch the word "Peas," using 3 strands of black embroidery thread. (See embroidery stitches in How-to Section.)

4. Cut out both label pieces and baste together, right sides out, about ¼" from the edge. Use invisible stitches to enclose the edge in red bias tape.

5. Pin the label in place on the jar, and appliqué with invisible stitches.

6. Cut a strip of red bias tape 6⅛" long. Press tape flat (it will be approximately ½" wide). Refer to pattern and baste tape in place on jar top. (Black tape will overlap both edges of the red.)

7. Cut a piece of black double-fold bias tape 19" long. This will be used as a flat trim, ¼" wide. To remove bulk, trim one side of tape, cutting ⅛" from center fold. (See Figure 1 under Salt and Pepper Potholders.) Discard narrow portion.

From trimmed tape, cut three strips, each 6⅛" long. Baste and hand-stitch in place on jar top.

8. Complete potholder, following Steps 7-10 under Salt and Pepper Potholders.

ACTUAL SIZE
pattern line is cutting line for fabric
broken lines indicate bias tape placement

black tape

red tape

black tape

black tape

MASON JAR POTHOLDER

Peas

red tape

black tape

You can make this cozy nap quilt just as thick and warm as you wish. As you can see, it's guaranteed to make you fall right to sleep . . . ZZZZ!

I wanted a truly cozy quilt—cozy even to the touch, so I used lightweight washable velour. Now, I know just what you're thinking—4¼ yards of 60″ fabric isn't your idea of a remnant. Right? Well, I chose to make the quilt using only two colors, so I did need very large pieces of fabric.

Actually, the quilt could be made from any collection of fabric scraps, making the letters in each row a different color or print. It could indeed be a true "scrap" quilt, but I didn't choose to make it that way.

When selecting your materials, remember that velour can be a fussy fabric. It marks easily, it slips around a lot, and it's very easy to turn the nap in the wrong direction when assembling the quilt.

An alternate cozy solution would be to use flannel or a combination of flannel and broadcloth (use the flannel for the letters and quilt back). Since flannel and broadcloth are narrow fabrics, you would need extra yardage and you would have to piece the back. The horizontal bands could be cut from the fabric length, since flannel nap wouldn't present the same problems you have with velour nap.

If you want a shorter quilt (this one measures 55x76″), eliminate the horizontal bands of border-colored fabric between the rows and use only one band of the background fabric. The quilt would then measure 55x68″.

Cozy Quilt

(color photo, page 77)

Materials

1 ³/₈ yards indigo lightweight
   washable velour, 60″ wide
4¼ yards terra cotta lightweight
   washable velour, 60″ wide
Thread to match fabric
Polyester quilt batting, 57x78″

Directions

If you use velour, you must keep nap direction consistent. As a reminder, use a white pencil to mark the top of each piece with a T on the wrong side of the fabric. Then keep all the Ts at the top as you assemble the blocks.

1. Make a complete A pattern by tracing the right and left sections from the book and butting them together on the dots (refer to sketch near the pattern piece sections).

Trace and cut actual-size patterns for the B and D pieces. Trace C on folded tracing paper to make a complete pattern (refer to sketch near pattern piece).

You will use these pattern pieces many times, so paste them to lightweight cardboard and cut them out.

2. On cardboard, draw and cut out these additional pattern

pieces (three rectangles and one square): E—4½x12½"; F—4½x4½"; G—4½x8½"; H—1½x12½". *Pattern lines are cutting lines for fabric; seam allowance is included.*

3. Determine the top of the indigo velour. Turn fabric over so wrong side faces you, and mark the top with a T. Refer to Figure 1 and, using a white pencil, trace pattern pieces face down on fabric.

Mark and label 22 B pieces, two D and two D-reversed pieces, nine F pieces, four G pieces and 25 H pieces. Also draw ten I pieces, each 1½x53½". (No pattern is given for this. Use your 1½"-wide H piece to help mark these long, 1½" strips.) Cut out fabric pieces.

4. From the terra cotta velour, cut off a 57" length; set aside the remaining section to use as the quilt back.

5. Turn the 57" length over, and mark the top with a T. Refer to Figure 2, and trace patterns face down on fabric. Mark and label 11 A pieces, two C pieces, 36 E pieces, and 14 F pieces. Cut out fabric pieces.

6. Refer to Figure 3. On the remaining section of terra cotta velour, mark, label and cut the following: six I pieces, each 1½x53½", two J pieces, each 1½x76½". (Use your 1½"-wide H pattern to help mark the I and J strips.)

7. As you piece the blocks, lightly press each seam after stitching. Refer to Figure 4, and begin with the letter "C" blocks. For each "C", use two terra cotta E pieces, one terra cotta F, and one indigo G. Join the F and G, and use as a horizontal row between the E pieces. Make four "C" blocks.

8. For each letter "O" block, use two terra cotta E pieces, two terra cotta F pieces, and one indigo F. Join a terra cotta F to each side of the indigo F to make a horizontal row, then stitch a terra cotta E above and below this row. Make three "O" blocks.

9. To make each "Z" block, use two terra cotta E pieces, one terra cotta A, and two indigo B pieces. (Keep top of each piece in position so that nap is consistent.) Make the center horizontal row, stitching an indigo B to each side of the terra cotta A. Then stitch a terra cotta E above and below. Make 11 "Z" blocks.

10. To make each "Y", use three terra cotta F pieces, three indigo F pieces, one indigo D, one indigo D-reversed and one terra cotta C piece. Join pieces to form horizontal rows, then join the rows. Make two "Y" blocks.

11. To assemble row 1, refer to Figure 4. Join blocks "C," "O," "Z" and "Y," placing an indigo H piece between each letter. Add an indigo H at the beginning and end of the row.

12. Repeat the procedure for row 2, spelling COZY. Row 3 spells COZZ. Row 4 is CZZZ, and row 5 is ZZZZ.

13. Join an indigo I piece to the top and bottom edge of each row. Lay out the rows in sequence from top to bottom. Stitch a terra cotta I piece between each row (to join them) and at top and bottom edges of quilt. Stitch a terra cotta J to both vertical edges.

14. Measure quilt top, and cut back from terra cotta velour to fit (about 55½x76½").

15. Working on a large flat surface, layer quilt pieces in this order: batting; quilt back (right side up); quilt top (wrong side up). Carefully line up edges and pin. Machine-stitch ¼" from the edge, leaving about 18" open along one side. Remove pins. Trim off corners.

16. Turn quilt right side out, gently pulling out the edges. Close opening with hand stitches.

17. Again working on a large flat surface, pin all around the outside edge of the quilt to position the seam line exactly on the edge. Baste close to edge, and remove pins. To keep the layers from shifting, pin or baste along the terra cotta I pieces between the rows.

18. Quilt directly on the seam line of the terra cotta border all around the quilt. Use a small running stitch.

19. Prepare to hand-quilt around each letter (not each block), and on each side of the terra cotta I strips between rows. Velour is too thick to put into a quilting hoop. If you don't have a quilting frame, spread the quilt out on the floor. Use lots of pins to flatten and smooth it; place pins parallel to, and on each side of, all seams to be quilted. This keeps the layers in place.

20. Begin quilting at the center of the quilt. Use a running stitch and work evenly toward all outside edges until finished.

Figure 1

Layout for indigo velour. Trace patterns face down on wrong side of fabric; seam allowance is included. Mark top of each piece before cutting. Note that 11 B pieces are in one one position, and 11 are rotated (but not reversed). This keeps nap in correct position for assembling quilt.

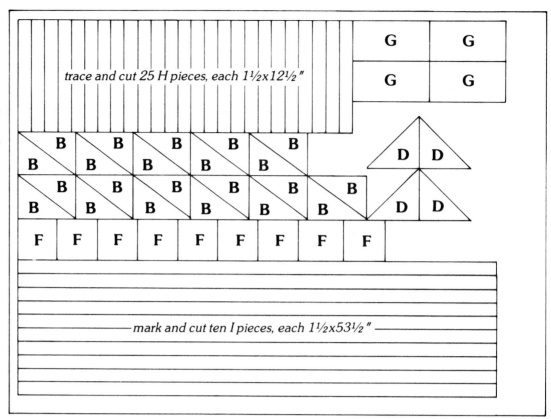

trace and cut 25 H pieces, each 1½x12½"

mark and cut ten I pieces, each 1½x53½"

Figure 2

Layout for terra cotta velour, 57" length. Trace patterns face down on wrong side of fabric; seam allowance is included.

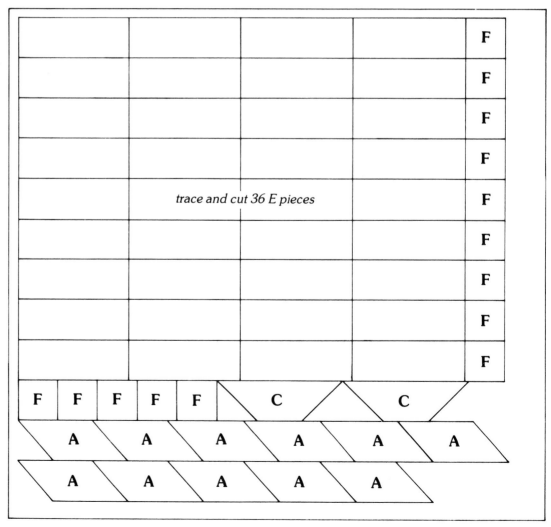

trace and cut 36 E pieces

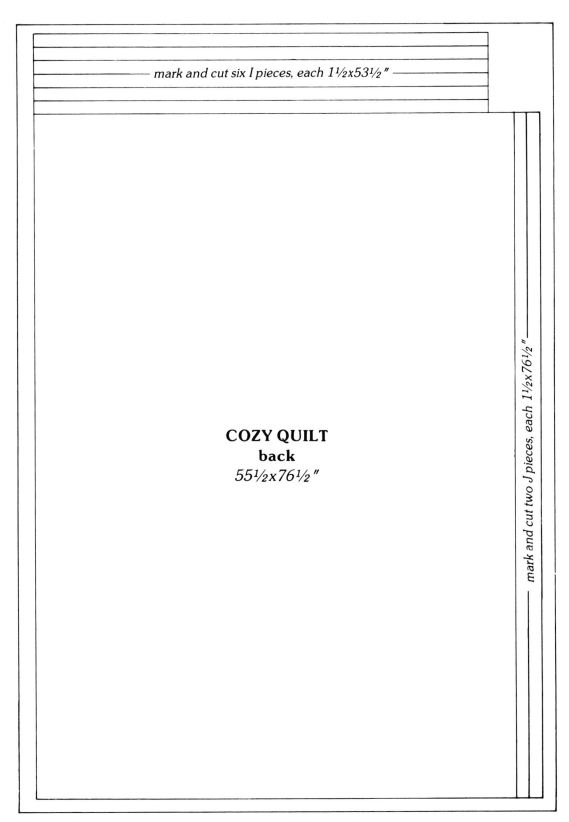

mark and cut six I pieces, each 1½x53½"

COZY QUILT
back
55½x76½"

mark and cut two J pieces, each 1½x76½"

Figure 3 *Layout for terra cotta velour, 96" length. Mark patterns on wrong side of fabric; seam allowance is included. Measure completed quilt top before cutting back.*

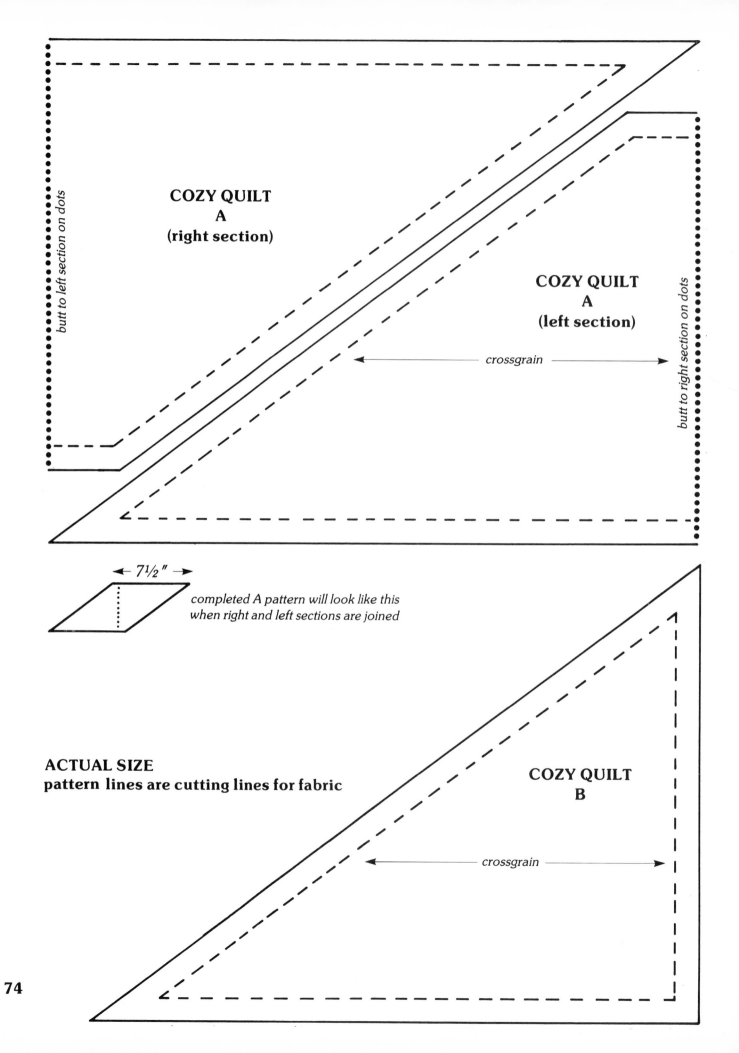

COZY QUILT
A
(right section)

butt to left section on dots

COZY QUILT
A
(left section)

crossgrain

butt to right section on dots

← 7½″ →

*completed A pattern will look like this
when right and left sections are joined*

ACTUAL SIZE
pattern lines are cutting lines for fabric

COZY QUILT
B

crossgrain

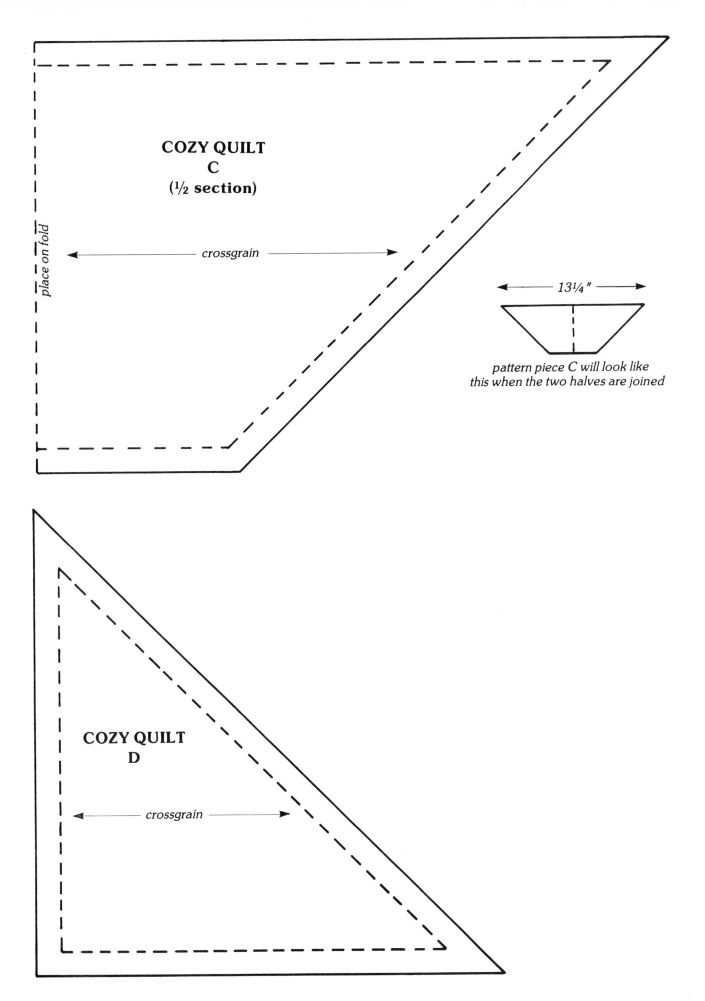

COZY QUILT
C
(½ section)

place on fold

crossgrain

13¼"

pattern piece C will look like
this when the two halves are joined

COZY QUILT
D

crossgrain

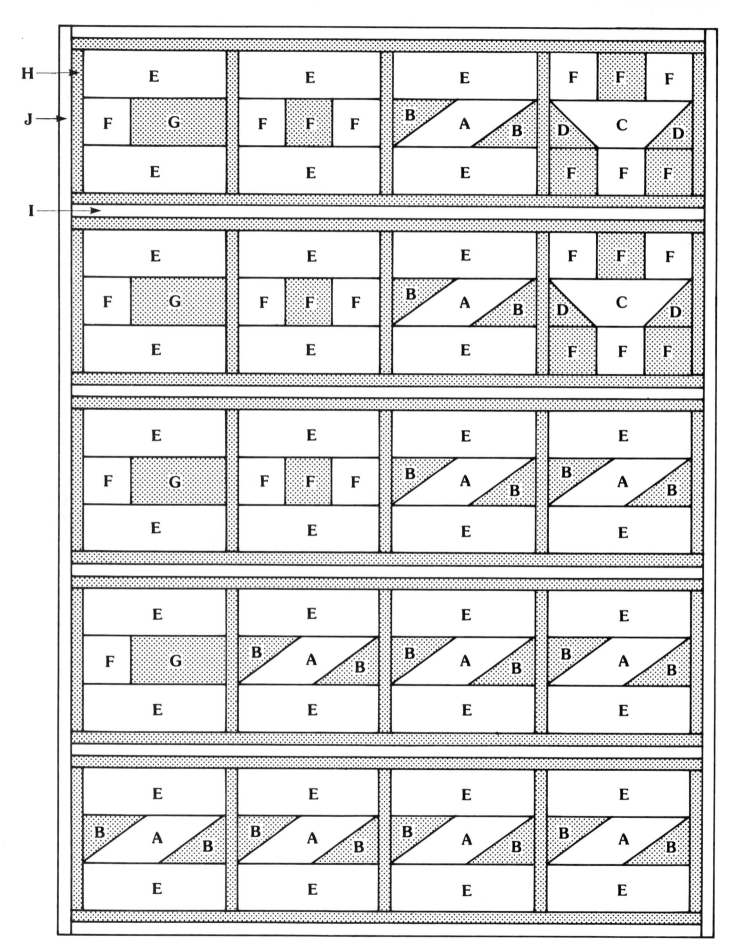

Figure 4 *Diagram of finished quilt.*

Snuggle under the Cozy Quilt, and you'll soon be snoozing (see page 70).

Potholders to perk up your kitchen masquerade as a jar of food, a warning that pots are H-O-T and salt and pepper shakers (see page 64).

Small squares of fabric form the Mosaic Patchwork Pillow designs, shown below. The elephant stands alone, but the cat has a little mouse sitting on his tail (see page 86).

Any meal gets a lift when you serve it on a colorful Puzzle Placemat, above (see page 88).

Three Christmas placemats add a festive touch to holiday meals. Choose the Star, top, Poinsettia, center, or Snowflake, below (see page 92).

These kitchen kittens hide all the paraphernalia that sits around that room collecting spots and dust. I have included cover patterns for a mixer, blender and toaster—and you can even make a mitten-type potholder to match.

If you are really cat-crazy, you could add a tea cozy and a cat-shaped fabric-covered bulletin board by changing the proportions of the patterns.

To make your collection of dotted, striped or calico cats, use quilted fabric; back it with non-woven interfacing for extra body. A collar of grosgrain ribbon edged with rickrack is stitched around the entire cover. I put ears and face on only one side, but you might choose to have cats on both front and back. If you do this, be sure to allow extra fabric for extra ears.

Kitchen Kittens

General Directions

These covers may not fit your appliances precisely. Check the appliance measurements first, and make adjustments on the pattern pieces. Add or subtract height at the bottom of the cat patterns, remembering to adjust side pieces, too. Add or subtract width at the center of the cats; also adjust width of side pieces as needed.

You'll need a zipper foot attachment for your sewing machine to stitch the cording.

1. Trace actual-size patterns, using folded tracing paper where indicated. Make a dot to mark center top of each front-and-back pattern. Mark dots for ear positions, and copy all design and trim lines.

2. Draw pattern for each side piece, following diagram; make a dot to mark the center on each long side, and copy trim lines. *Pattern lines are cutting lines for fabric; seam allowance is included.*

3. Pin patterns to wrong side of quilted fabric and trace around them. Cut one front, one back, one side piece and four ears for each cover.

4. On right side of fabric, transfer features to front piece, and transfer placement lines for ribbon collar to all pieces. (See transfer directions in How-to Section.)

5. Embroider, using six strands of embroidery thread. Chain-stitch black eyes and brows,

white whiskers and red mouth. Satin-stitch the white nose. (See How-to Section for embroidery stitches.)

6. Cut interfacing for front, back and side pieces (but not ears), using the same patterns. Mark center point on both long edges of the side piece and on the top of both front and back. Pin and baste interfacing to wrong side of fabric pieces.

7. Cut ribbon and rickrack to proper lengths. Position ribbon so it overlaps rickrack along each edge, then tack rickrack points to ribbon with tiny hand stitches. Pin ribbon pieces to cover front, back and side pieces, and hand-stitch in place.

8. Cut pieces of corded piping to required length for front and back, then trim seam allowance to $1/4''$, if necessary. Baste piping to curved edges of front and back (raw edges of piping should be even with raw edges of fabric). Machine-stitch on seam line, using zipper foot attachment. To secure quilting threads, machine-stitch the single layers of front and back, about $1/8''$ from lower edge.

9. Cut corded piping to proper length for ears. Trim seam allowance to $1/4''$ and clip at intervals to help it curve. Position piping on each ear front along the two curves forming the ear point. Baste, then machine-stitch on the seam line.

Pin ear back to ear front, right sides together (piping in be-

tween); baste and stitch on the two sides with piping. Trim off seam allowance at tip of ear; grade and clip seam allowances.

Turn ear right side out. Pin and machine-stitch lower edge along seam line, then clip to stitching line.

10. Pin each ear in place between dots on head (seam edges will be even and tip of ear will point toward face). Baste and machine-stitch on seam line.

11. To secure quilting threads on the side piece, machine-stitch the short straight edges about $1/8''$ from the edge.

Pin side piece to kitten front and back pieces, matching ribbons and center dots. Baste and machine-stitch. Trim interfacing close to seam line and clip curves. Turn right side out.

12. Cover lower edge with bias tape, and hand-stitch in place. Tack bell to front of kitten.

Mixer Cover

Approximately $10^1/2$x12x$12^1/4''$ high. Adjust pattern to fit your appliance, following suggestions given under General Directions.

Materials

Quilted yellow calico, 31x35" (35" is the length); matching thread
Non-woven heavy interfacing, 25x35"
2½ yards red corded piping
1⅜ yards blue grosgrain ribbon, ⅝" wide; matching thread
2¾ yards white baby rickrack

Embroidery thread, 1½ yards each: red, black, white

1⅓ yards red double-fold bias tape, ¼" wide

Large jingle bell

Directions

1. Follow General Directions, Steps 1-6. (In Step 1, add 2½" below broken line at bottom of front-and-back pattern.) See Figure 1 for side piece measurements.

2. Cut ribbon as follows: two side pieces, each 13"; one front and one back piece, each 11½". Cut rickrack pieces as follows: four side pieces, each 13"; two front and two back pieces, each 11½". Complete Step 7 under General Directions.

3. Cut two corded piping pieces, each 34" long. Complete Step 8 under General Directions.

4. Cut two corded piping pieces, each 9" long. Complete Steps 9-12 under General Directions.

Blender Cover

Approximately 7½x9x15" high. Adjust the pattern to fit your appliance, following suggestions given under General Directions.

Materials

Quilted yellow calico, 19x39½" (39½" is the length); matching thread

Non-woven heavy interfacing, 19x38"

2½ yards red corded piping

1⅛ yards blue grosgrain ribbon, ⅝" wide; matching thread

2¼ yards white baby rickrack

Embroidery thread, 1½ yards each: red, black, white

1⅛ yards red double-fold bias tape, ¼" wide

Large jingle bell

Directions

1. Follow General Directions, Steps 1-6. (In Step 1, add 5½" below broken line at bottom of front-and-back pattern.) See Figure 2 for side piece measurements.

2. Cut ribbon pieces as follows: two side pieces, each 10"; one front and one back piece, each 8¾". Cut rickrack pieces as follows: four side pieces, each 10"; two front and two back pieces, each 8¾". Complete Step 7 under General Directions.

3. Cut two corded piping pieces, each 37¼". Complete Step 8 under General Directions.

4. Cut two corded piping pieces, each 8". Complete Steps 9-12 under General Directions.

Toaster Cover

Approximately 6⅜x11x8⅜" high. Adjust pattern to fit your appliance, following suggestions given under General Directions.

Materials

Quilted yellow calico, 19x23" (23" is the length); matching thread

Non-woven heavy interfacing, 19x22"

1⅝ yards red corded piping

1⅛ yards blue grosgrain ribbon, ⅝" wide; matching thread

2¼ yards white baby rickrack

Embroidery thread, 1 yard each: red, black, white

1 yard red double-fold bias tape, ¼" wide

Large jingle bell

Directions

1. Follow General Directions, Steps 1-6. See Figure 3 for side piece measurements.

2. Cut ribbon pieces as follows: two side pieces, each 12"; one front and one back piece, each 7½". Cut rickrack pieces as follows: four side pieces, each 12"; two front and two back pieces, each 7½". Complete Step 7 under General Directions.

3. Cut two corded piping pieces, each 22¼". Complete Step 8 under General Directions.

4. Cut two corded piping pieces, each 6". Complete Steps 9-12 under General Directions.

Potholder

Materials

Quilted yellow calico, 15x21" (21" is the length); matching thread

Polyester quilt batting, 9½x15"

1 yard red corded piping

7½" blue grosgrain ribbon, ⅝" wide; matching thread

15" white baby rickrack

Embroidery thread, 1 yard each: red, black, white

14" red double-fold bias tape, ¼" wide

Large jingle bell

Directions

1. Trace pattern pieces for front and back and for ear, referring to Step 1 under General Directions. (Pattern for potholder is same as that for toaster cover.)

2. Cut four ears, two fronts and two backs from quilted fabric, and one front and one back from batting. Transfer trim lines and embroider face (see Step 5 under General Directions).

Layer pieces for front and back in this order: fabric (right side down), batting, fabric (right side up). Baste layers together and treat as one piece of fabric.

3. Cut one ribbon strip 7½" and two rickrack strips, each 7½". Follow Step 7 under General Directions and apply collar to front only.

4. Cut one corded piping piece, 22". Complete Step 8 under General Directions, adding cording to front only.

5. Cut two corded piping pieces, each 6". Complete Steps 9-10 under General Directions.

6. Pin and stitch potholder front and back together. Grade and clip seam. Turn to right side.

7. Cover lower raw edge with bias tape. Tack on bell. Add a hanging loop, if desired.

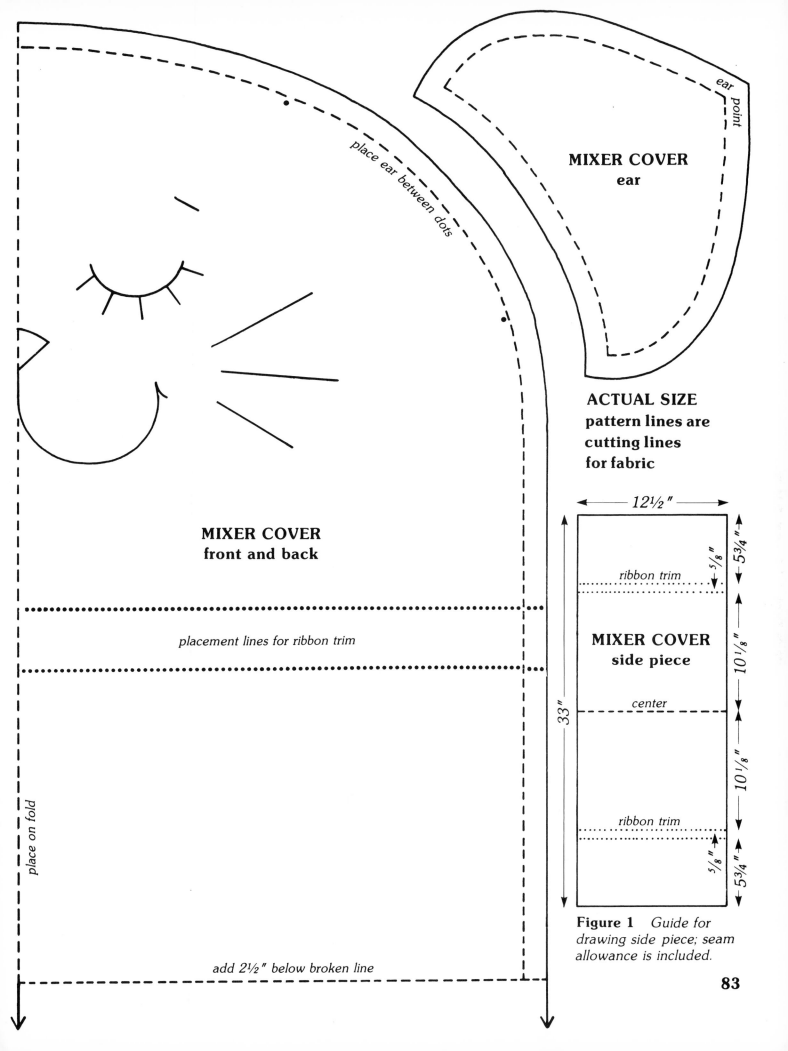

place ear between dots

MIXER COVER
ear

ear point

ACTUAL SIZE
pattern lines are
cutting lines
for fabric

MIXER COVER
front and back

placement lines for ribbon trim

place on fold

add 2½" below broken line

12½"

ribbon trim

5/8"

5¾"

MIXER COVER
side piece

10⅛"

center

33"

10⅛"

ribbon trim

5/8"

5¾"

Figure 1 *Guide for drawing side piece; seam allowance is included.*

ACTUAL SIZE
pattern lines are cutting lines for fabric

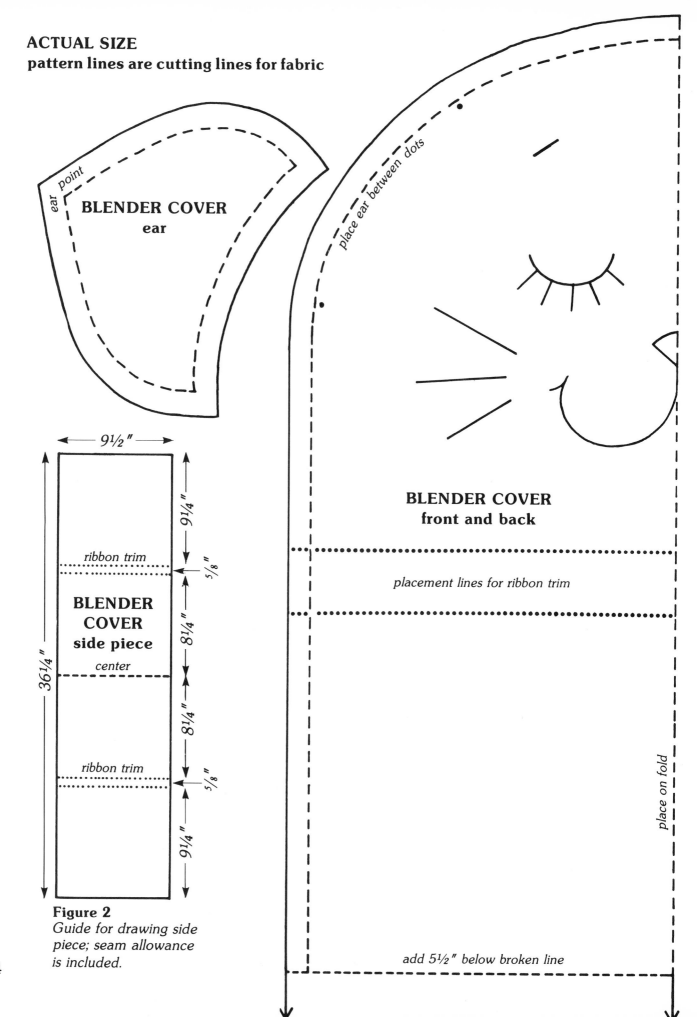

BLENDER COVER
ear

ear point

BLENDER COVER
front and back

place ear between dots

placement lines for ribbon trim

place on fold

add 5½" below broken line

9½"

9¼"

5/8"

ribbon trim

**BLENDER COVER
side piece**

center

8¼"

8¼"

36¼"

ribbon trim

5/8"

9¼"

Figure 2
*Guide for drawing side
piece; seam allowance
is included.*

84

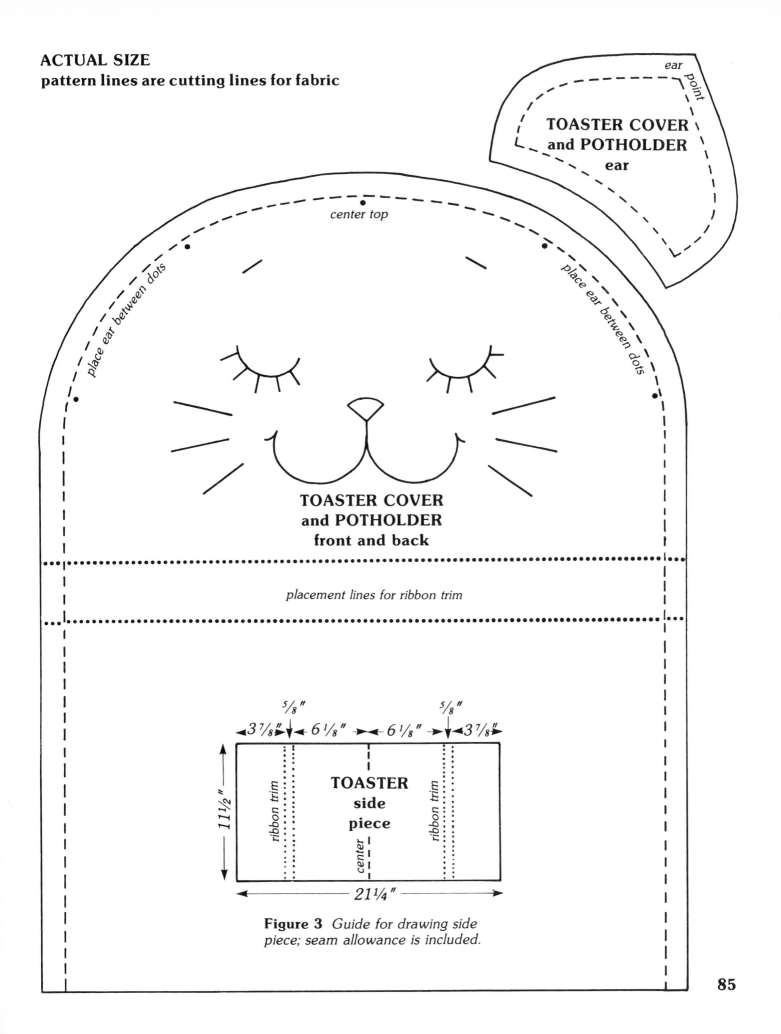

ACTUAL SIZE
pattern lines are cutting lines for fabric

ear
point

TOASTER COVER
and POTHOLDER
ear

center top

place ear between dots

place ear between dots

TOASTER COVER
and POTHOLDER
front and back

placement lines for ribbon trim

5/8" 5/8"
3 7/8" 6 1/8" 6 1/8" 3 7/8"

ribbon trim

TOASTER
side
piece

center

ribbon trim

11 1/2"

21 1/4"

Figure 3 *Guide for drawing side piece; seam allowance is included.*

85

Both these pillows are good beginner projects. Even though they take some time, there are no patterns to copy or enlarge.

Designs are made by combining same-size squares in a variety of colors and prints. The pillows are easy to make, but it's essential to be accurate when measuring, cutting, and stitching each individual square.

For the cat design, keep the background and cat fabrics close in value—the darker, the better, I think—and then the ears won't look like two little blocks (which they are!). Dark colors will also make your cat look more mysterious. If you don't like black, try a dark brown or indigo.

If you just don't need another pillow, one of these designs might be used for the front of a padded and lined tote bag. Or you could enlarge the squares to make a 36"- or 45"-square replacement pad for a playpen, with ribbon ties at each corner.

Perhaps you've been looking for a simple-to-sew quilt pattern. Think about using one of these designs, increasing the size of the squares to make a puffy coverlet.

Mosaic Patchwork Pillows

Elephant Pillow

(color photo, page 78)

Materials

Red and white narrow stripe, 4x23½"
Red and white check, 7x19"
Red and white floral print, 7x19"
Blue and white floral print, 8½x25"
White scrap, 7x25"
Blue and white check, 17x17", for back
Thread to match or blend with fabrics
Embroidery thread: ½ yard blue, 1½ yards white
Blue button, ½" diameter
Polyester stuffing

Directions

Finished pillow measures approximately 16x16".

l. There are no patterns for this project. Measure and draw 1½" squares directly on the back of each fabric; this dimension includes ¼" seam allowance. (Using a drawing board with a T-square and triangle probably provides the most accurate results. Or you could make a cardboard template.)

Prepare the following number of squares: 30 red and white stripe, 43 red and white check, 46 red and white floral, 77 blue and white floral, and 60 white. Cut out squares.

2. Arrange squares in order on a flat surface, following placement guide. Pin and stitch squares together in horizontal rows, making ¼" seams. Press all seams flat. Join horizontal rows to complete pillow front.

3. Embroider mouth, checking guide for placement. Use four strands of blue embroidery thread and chain-stitch on the seam line. (See embroidery stitches in How-to Section.)

4. Sew on button eye, or substitute an embroidered eye if pillow is for a child younger than three.

5. To make tail, cut three 16" lengths of white embroidery thread. Thread needle with one length to make a double strand, and stitch through pillow front at tail spot; pull thread halfway through fabric. Cut needle free. Attach all three lengths of thread in this way to make 12 thread ends, each 4" long. Divide into three sections and braid to 1½" length. Knot securely and trim tassel to 1¼".

6. Check dimensions of pieced pillow front, and cut a pillow back 16½x16½" (or adjusted to fit front) from blue and white checked fabric. Pin to pillow front, right sides together. Stitch around the outside, making ¼" seams and leaving a 4" opening on one side. Clip off corners and turn pillow right side out. Stuff, and close opening with invisible hand stitches.

Cat and Mouse Pillow

Materials

Black and white pin stripe, 12½x15½"
  (or ¼ yard, 44" wide)
Black, white, red, green floral print,
  9½x35" (or ¼ yard, 44" wide)
White scrap, 9½x17½" (or ¼ yard,
  44" wide)
Red scrap, 2x5"
Black and white dot, 17x17", for back
Thread to match or blend with fabrics
Embroidery thread: ¾ yard white,
  ½ yard black
2 green buttons, ⅝" diameter
Polyester stuffing

Directions

Finished pillow measures
approximately 16x16".

l. Refer to Step 1 of Elephant
Pillow. Prepare and cut out the
following 1½" squares: 74
stripe, 115 floral, 64 white and
3 red.

2. Join squares, following
Step 2 under Elephant Pillow.

3. Embroider eyes on mouse,
following placement guide. Use
two strands of black thread and
a satin stitch; make eyes about
⅛" in diameter. Chain-stitch tail
on the seam lines, using four
strands of white. (See embroidery stitches in How-to Section.)

4. Sew button eyes on cat, or
substitute embroidery if pillow is
intended for someone under the
age of three.

5. Cut a back section
16½x16½" (or adjusted to fit
front) from black and white dot
fabric. Finish pillow, following
Step 6 under Elephant Pillow.

ELEPHANT PILLOW
placement guide

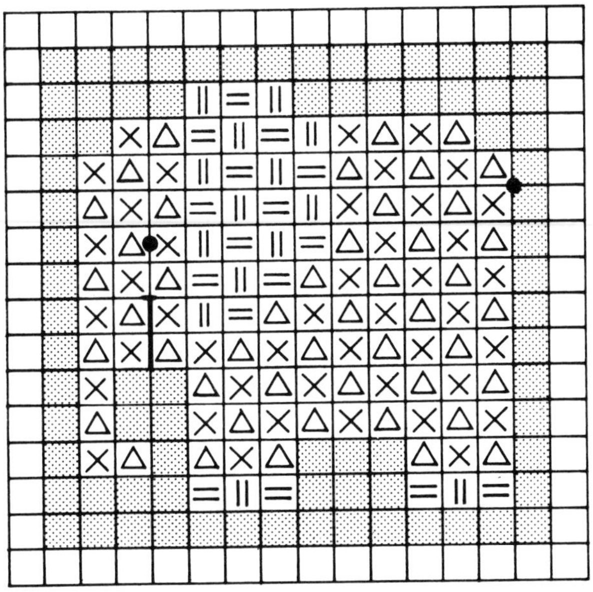

☒ blue and white floral

= red and white narrow stripe

△ red and white floral

☒ red and white check

☐ white

CAT and MOUSE PILLOW
placement guide

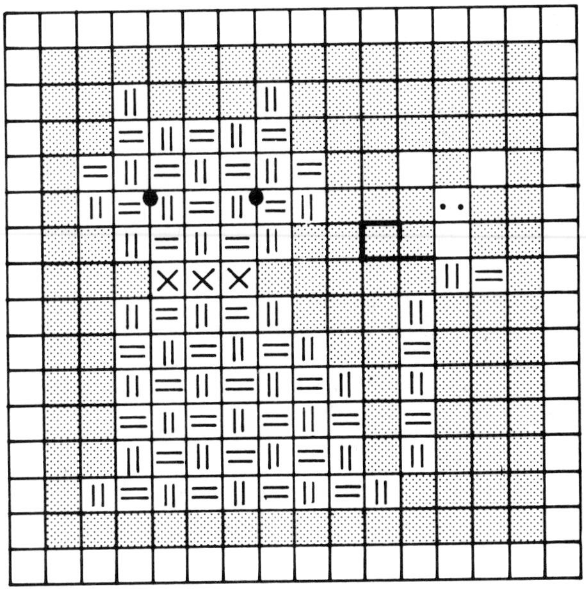

= black and white pin stripe

☒ black, white, red, green floral

☒ red

☐ white

EACH SQUARE = 1 SQUARE INCH (on finished pillows)

Use a whole handful of your scraps—both solids and prints—to make a group of these puzzle placemats. There's really no need to have them match, and if you use a variety of prints within each mat, your table could have all the charm of an old-fashioned crazy quilt.

Stay away from fabrics that fray easily, and do use the fusible web for easy assembly and *neat results. The web is expensive, but you can overlap the remnants and use up every little bit. The wide zigzag stitches use up a lot of thread, but perhaps you can find inexpensive large spools of polyester thread at a discount store, as I often do. The thread quality isn't very important in this project.*

Puzzle Placemat

(color photo, page 79)

Materials (for each mat)

Scraps, 7¾x7¾" each: brilliant pink, gold, green, blue, lavender, orange
Fusible web, 15½x23¼" (cut into six 7¾x7¾" pieces)
White scrap, 20x28"
Polyester quilt batting, 13½x19¼"
Large spool white thread (225 yards)

Directions

1. Patterns for puzzle pieces are actual size. Copy pieces A, B and C on tracing paper; label, and cut out. To make a B-reversed pattern, flip the B piece over and trace it again, omitting the ⅛" overlap on the straight side as indicated on the pattern in the book. Cut out.

2. Make a full-size pattern for the placemat front and back by drawing a 13x18¾" rectangle. Draw a ¾" border inside the edge. Set pattern aside.

3. For puzzle pieces, *pattern lines are cutting lines for fabric.* Pin each puzzle piece to right side of fabric and trace around it. Use the A piece to draw one pink, one green and one lavender. Use the B piece to draw one gold. Use the B-reversed piece to draw one blue. Use the C piece to draw one orange. Do not cut fabric.

4. Remove patterns and pin a square of fusible web to the wrong side of each fabric square. Before cutting, baste just inside each puzzle shape (about ¹⁄₁₆"), using white thread. Cut out shapes and set aside.

5. For placemat front and back, *pattern lines are stitching lines; add seam allowance when cutting fabric.* On the wrong side of folded white fabric, trace around placemat rectangle. Lightly mark border on the top fabric layer with pencil. Cut out fabric, adding ¼" seam allowance on all edges. Use the same pattern to cut a batting piece, adding ¼" seam allowance.

6. Transfer border marking to right side of fabric (one layer only), using large bastings; this layer will be the placemat front.

7. Refer to Figure 1, and position puzzle pieces on the front in this order: 1. B (gold) at center top, 2. B-reversed (blue) at lower left, and 3. C (orange) at lower right. Pin in place within the bor- der. Overlap these pieces with: 4. A (pink) at top left, 5. A (green) at top right, and 6. A (lavender) at center bottom.

8. Lightly touch the iron to a few spots on each puzzle piece to secure. Remove pins. Cover work with a cloth and press. Turn work over and press the back. Allow fabric to cool. Test adhesion and press again if nec-necessary.

9. Work on a flat surface and layer pieces in this order: batting, placemat back (right side up), placemat front (wrong side up). Carefully line up edges and pin. Trim batting, if necessary. Machine-stitch ¼" from edge, leaving 4" opening at center top. Remove pins. Trim off corners.

10. Turn mat right side out, gently pushing out corners. Close top opening with hand stitches. Lightly press edges.

11. Place pins within each puzzle piece to keep work from shifting as you stitch. Set your machine for a wide, close zigzag stitch, and machine-stitch over raw edges of puzzle pieces. (You may want to go over seams twice to obtain a solid satin stitch.)

PUZZLE PLACEMAT
A

ACTUAL SIZE
pattern line is cutting line for fabric

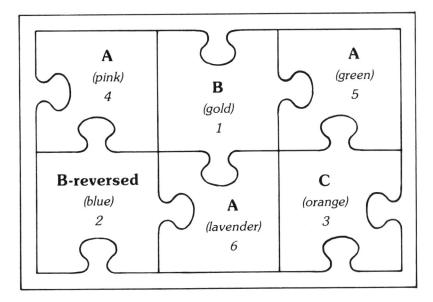

Figure 1 *Placement guide for puzzle pieces.*

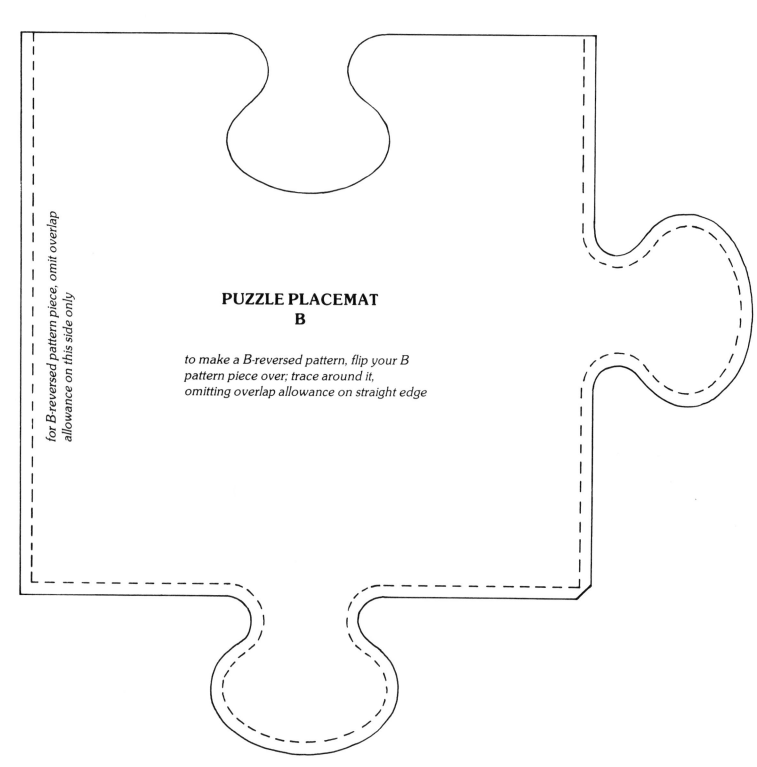

for B-reversed pattern piece, omit overlap allowance on this side only

PUZZLE PLACEMAT
B

to make a B-reversed pattern, flip your B pattern piece over; trace around it, omitting overlap allowance on straight edge

ACTUAL SIZE

pattern line is cutting line for fabric

broken line indicates where adjoining pieces will overlap

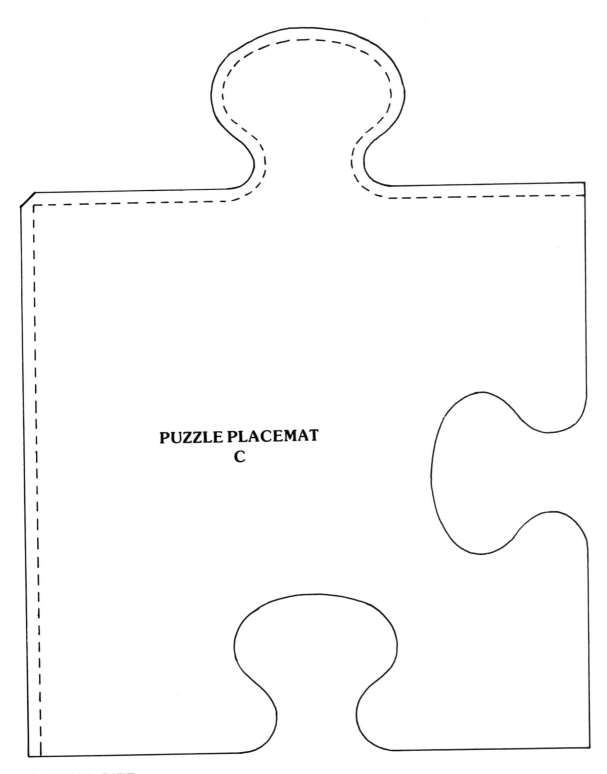

**PUZZLE PLACEMAT
C**

ACTUAL SIZE
pattern line is cutting line for fabric

broken line indicates where adjoining pieces will overlap

Three traditional holiday symbols are used in these Christmas placemats. I wanted the look of big, bold graphic shapes instead of fussy little motifs.

The poinsettia and star are pieced like patchwork blocks and are, in fact, based on quilt patterns. The snowflake is cut as one large hexagon, and the design is appliquéd with twill tape.

If you're short on time and it's too much work to make enough placemats for everyone at your Christmas table, try doing just one as a centerpiece mat. Each of them looks quite festive with a single silver candlestick and a small silver bowl holding candy or holly.

You might discover uses of your own for these designs. You could use them to make pillows or chair cushions, or just hang them up as wall art. The star might even be used as a floor target for a button-toss game.

If you're really adventurous, you could also enlarge these mat designs to make great circular tablecloths.

Christmas Placemats

Star Placemat
(color photo, page 79)

Materials (for each mat)

Yellow-orange scrap, 7x9"
Orange scrap, 6½x17"
Red scrap, 11½x13½"
Magenta scrap, 7x25"
Purple scrap, 18x29"
Thread to match or blend with fabrics
Colorless nylon thread for quilting (optional)
Polyester batting, 18x18"

Directions

Heavy fabrics are not suitable because they will form bulky seams at center of mat. If you use sheer fabric, you may wish to back completed mat front with a circle of white batiste before adding batting.

Colorless nylon thread is helpful for quilting the mat since so many different colored fabrics are used. You'll need a compass for drawing the back pattern.

1. Trace actual-size A, B, C, D and E patterns and cut out. Transfer the dot on piece A. (Dotted points will always be at center when you assemble mat.) For the mat back pattern, draw and cut out a 17" circle. *Pattern*

lines are stitching lines; add seam allowance when cutting fabric.

2. Trace around pattern shapes (face down) on the wrong side of fabrics; add ¼" seam allowance all around when you cut them out. From yellow-orange, cut five A pieces and five A-reversed pieces (flip the A piece over and trace around the reverse side); lightly place the dot on each piece within the seam allowance.

From orange scrap, cut five B pieces and five B-reversed pieces. From red, cut five C pieces and five C-reversed pieces. From magenta, cut five D pieces and five D-reversed pieces. From purple, cut five E pieces and one back circle piece.

3. Use the back circle pattern to cut one batting piece, adding ¼" seam allowance.

4. Lay the front fabric pieces in position on a flat surface, right side up (see Figure 1). Make sure dotted points of yellow-orange A pieces are at the center.

5. Work with one wedge-shaped strip, using an A, B, C and D piece (see Figure 2). With pins, carefully match up traced seam lines, and join a yellow-orange A to an orange B, right

sides together. Join this A/B piece to a red C. Join piece A/B/C to a magenta D. Press all seams flat. Complete 10 wedge-shaped strips (five strips will have shapes reversed).

6. Join an A/B/C/D strip to an A/B/C/D-reversed strip (see Figure 3). Take an E border piece, clip into the seam allowance on the inner curve every ¼", then pin and stitch to the large wedge. Press seam toward border. Repeat to make five more units. Join all units to complete the circle (Figure 1).

7. Baste layer of batting to wrong side of mat front. Place pins within fabric shapes to keep layers from shifting. To quilt, machine-stitch around each star on the seam lines.

8. Pin back to front, right sides together. Machine-stitch ¼" from the edge, leaving a 3" opening for turning. Clip or pink seam. Turn mat right side out, and close opening with invisible stitches.

9. Place pins around the outside, making sure seam line is precisely on the edge. Baste and press edge flat. Machine-quilt inner edge of purple border on seam line.

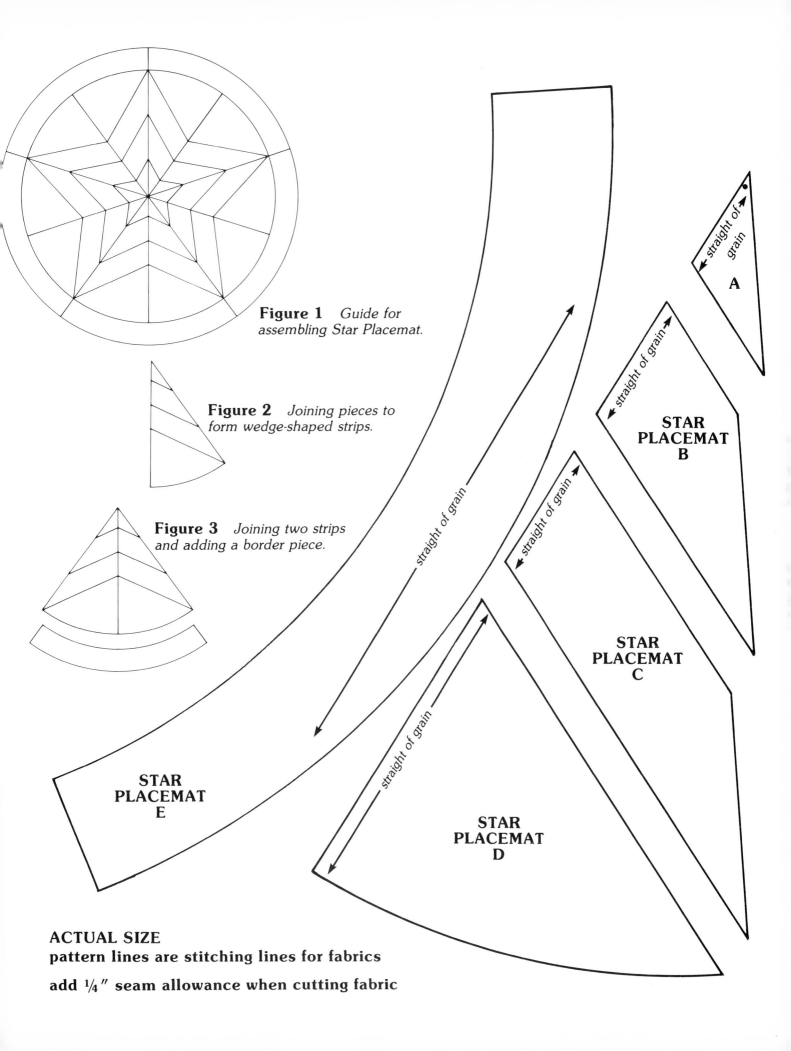

Figure 1 *Guide for assembling Star Placemat.*

Figure 2 *Joining pieces to form wedge-shaped strips.*

Figure 3 *Joining two strips and adding a border piece.*

straight of grain

straight of grain

straight of grain

straight of grain

straight of grain

A

STAR PLACEMAT B

STAR PLACEMAT C

STAR PLACEMAT E

STAR PLACEMAT D

ACTUAL SIZE

pattern lines are stitching lines for fabrics

add ¼″ seam allowance when cutting fabric

Poinsettia Placemat
(color photo, page 79)

Materials (for each mat)

Yellow scrap, 3½x3½"
Red small dot scrap, 10x11"
Red large dot scrap, 10x11"
Green scrap (print, stripe or solid), 10x22"
Solid green scrap, 19x19", for back
Thread to match or blend with fabrics
Polyester quilt batting, 19x19"

Directions

1. Trace actual-size patterns A, B and C, and cut out. To make a complete back pattern, refer to Figure 1, and trace D eight times; cut out. *Pattern lines are stitching lines; add seam allowance when cutting fabric.*

2. Trace around pattern shapes on wrong side of fabric. Trace piece A once on yellow fabric, and mark dots. Trace B four times on each of the two red print fabrics to make eight pieces.

Trace C 16 times on green fabric. (If using a stripe, trace eight C and eight C-reversed so that stripe will be in correct position on finished mat.) Trace complete back pattern once on solid green fabric. Cut out all fabric pieces, adding ¼" seam allowance.

3. Refer to Figure 2. Join a green C piece to each side of the red B pieces, right sides together. Press seams flat. Join all these units, alternating the red print fabrics; this makes a petal and leaf ring. Press the seams flat.

4. Pin the ring of petals and leaves to yellow center A, right

sides together, matching dots on A to seams. (It helps to first clip into seam allowance on the red fabric.) Baste, easing in fullness. Stitch. Lightly press seam away from center.

5. Use complete back pattern to cut quilt batting, adding ¼" seam allowance.

6. Pin and baste batting to wrong side of mat front. Place pins inside petals, leaves, and center to keep fabric from shifting. To quilt, machine-stitch around center A and between the B petals (but not into the green leaf sections).

7. Pin mat front to mat back, right sides together, carefully lining up edges. Machine-stitch ¼" from edge on the seam line; leave one V-shaped leaf section unstitched for turning. Clip into V areas and clip off points; trim batting close to stitching line.

8. Turn mat right side out,

and close opening with hand stitches. Pin around the outside to position seam line exactly on the edge. Also pin around center to keep layers from shifting as you quilt. Machine-quilt center and petals on seam lines.

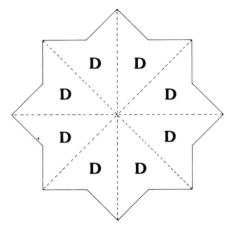

Figure 1 *Guide for drawing complete backing pattern.*

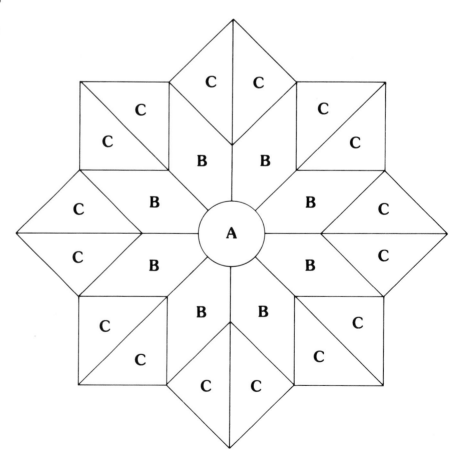

Figure 2 *Guide for assembling Poinsettia Placemat.*

94

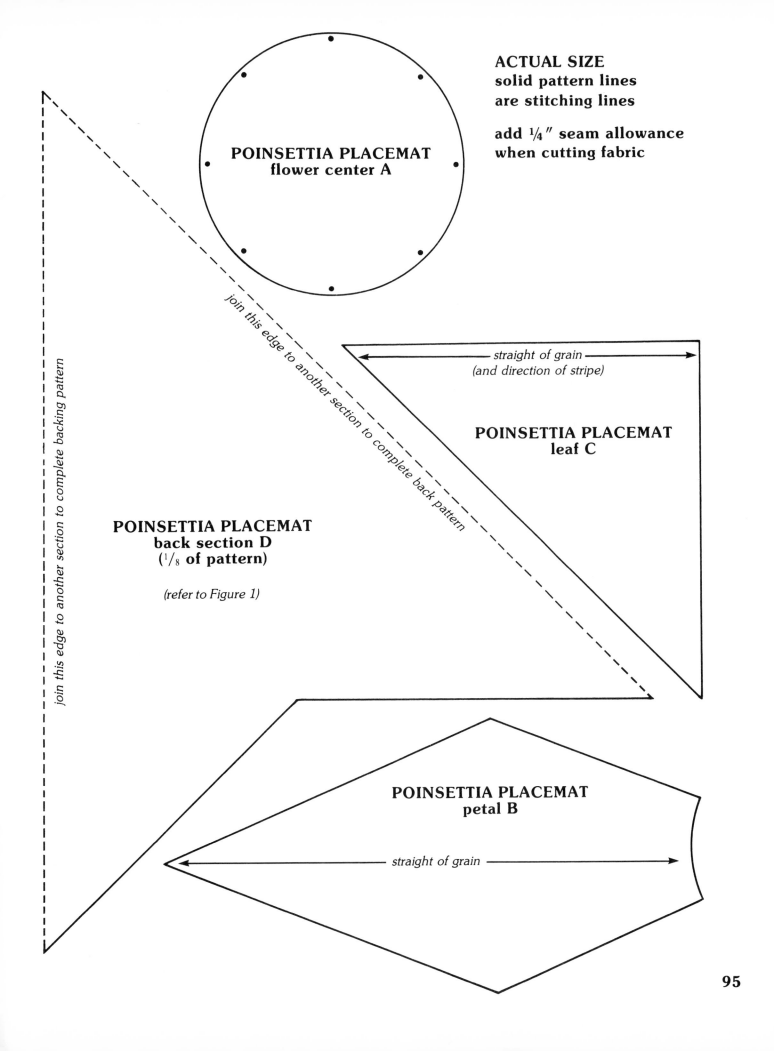

POINSETTIA PLACEMAT
flower center A

ACTUAL SIZE
solid pattern lines
are stitching lines

add ¼″ seam allowance
when cutting fabric

join this edge to another section to complete back pattern

straight of grain
(and direction of stripe)

POINSETTIA PLACEMAT
leaf C

join this edge to another section to complete backing pattern

POINSETTIA PLACEMAT
back section D
(¹/₈ **of pattern**)

(refer to Figure 1)

POINSETTIA PLACEMAT
petal B

straight of grain

95

Snowflake Placemat
(color photo, page 79)

For a quicker and less expensive version of this placemat, omit the twill tape and zigzag white stitches on both edges of the snowflake design.

If you don't have a zigzag feature on your sewing machine, use large straight machine stitches with buttonhole twist. The effect will be much more delicate than with twill tape.

Materials

Blue fabric, 17x37"; blue thread
5 yards white twill tape, ¾" wide; white thread
Polyester quilt batting, 17x18½"
6 large white fringe balls, 1" diameter (optional)

Directions

1. Trace quarter section pattern of snowflake, copying all inside design lines for tape placement. Add three more sections (two reversed) to make complete mat front pattern (see Figure 1).

You will use this same pattern (without design lines) to cut back and batting. If you are making a number of these mats, make a second pattern and glue it to lightweight cardboard; cut out the negative (blue) areas to make a template. *Pattern lines are stitching lines; add seam allowance when cutting fabric.*

2. Trace around pattern on wrong side of fabric; make one front and one back piece for each placemat. Cut out, adding ¼" seam allowance.

To transfer design lines to right side of front piece, use template and a white pencil, or

(without a template) pin pattern in place and use dressmaker's carbon, tracing wheel and ruler. (See How-to Section for transferring design lines.)

3. Use front pattern to trace one batting piece. Cut out, adding ¼" seam allowance.

4. Cut twill tape A, B, and C into lengths indicated on pattern guides. Cut six A strips, six B strips and 12 C strips. In addition, cut three D strips, each 18" long (no guide is given).

5. Work on a flat surface and start placing the A strips. Pin and baste each strip to the mat, folding tape to create points of the snowflake. (Tape ends will butt against adjoining A strips, and raw ends will be covered later by the D strips.) Pin and baste B and C strips in place.

6. Baste batting to wrong side of mat front, placing stitches around edge and on tapes to keep fabric and tapes in place.

7. Machine-stitch both edges of each tape strip. (This quilts the mat.)

8. Pin and stitch D strips to mat, one strip at a time.

9. Pin mat front to back, right sides together. Machine-stitch around the outside, leaving a 4" opening on one side. Turn right side out, and close opening with invisible hand stitches.

10. Place pins along edges, making sure seam line is exactly on the edge. Baste close to edge, then press edges flat. Remove bastings.

11. Tack a fringe ball to each point of mat if you wish.

SNOWFLAKE PLACEMAT

SNOWFLAKE PLACEMAT

inner fold

outer fold

twill tape guide A

inner fold

outer fold

twill tape guide B

SNOWFLAKE PLACEMAT
twill tape guide C

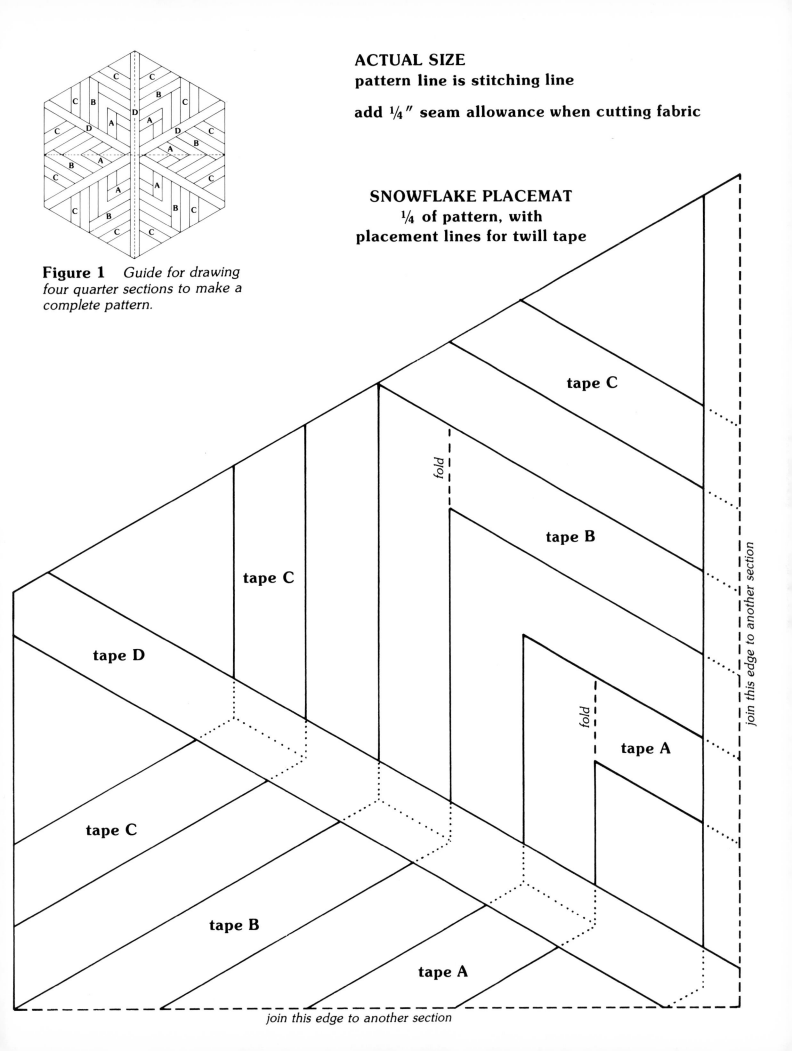

ACTUAL SIZE
pattern line is stitching line

add ¼″ seam allowance when cutting fabric

SNOWFLAKE PLACEMAT
¼ of pattern, with
placement lines for twill tape

Figure 1 *Guide for drawing four quarter sections to make a complete pattern.*

tape C

fold

tape B

tape C

tape D

fold

tape A

tape C

tape B

tape A

join this edge to another section

join this edge to another section

Exactly one week before Christmas I decided it was now or never concerning the Santa Stocking.

Most of the time I work best under pressure— perhaps you do, too. What really provided the motivation, however, was showing the sketch to my three-year-old and saying, "I promise."

The race was on!

I did finish it, but in typical three-year-old fashion, my little one changed her mind on Christmas Eve and decided she would rather use her old stocking from last year. At that moment the Santa Stocking became a door decoration.

When you're gathering materials to make this, do use a good quality red felt. The trim colors can be lightweight, but the red felt must be thick and sturdy or it won't survive the years of investigation. Use a double layer of the red if you have only very thin felt.

Santa Stocking

(color photo, page 115)

Materials

Sturdy red felt, 12x33"
Light pink felt, 2½x4"
Dark green felt, 2¾x5½"
Light grey felt, 2½x10¼"
White felt, 6½x8"
3-ply crewel yarn: 7 yards dark grey,
  5 yards white, 1½ yards green,
  2 yards red, 1 yard medium pink
Polyester stuffing (optional)
White fringe ball, ⅝" diameter
Plastic curtain ring, ¾" diameter

Directions

Finished stocking measures about 11¾x17".

1. Trace actual-size quarter sections of stocking pattern, butting them together on dotted lines to make a complete stocking front (see Figure 1). Copy placement lines for bricks, snowflakes and sleeve trim. (After cutting the felt front, you can use this same pattern for the untrimmed stocking back if you cut off the hat, as in Figure 2.)

2. Trace separate patterns for beard, mustache, face (with features), mittens and chimney top (with snowflakes). *Pattern lines are cutting lines for felt.*

3. On right side of red felt, trace one stocking front and one stocking back.

On front piece, transfer details by first piercing pattern with a large needle (such as that used for crewel embroidery), then pushing a soft pencil into each hole to mark felt. (When you transfer snowflake and sleeve details, mark the lines only. You can place the French knots by eye when you embroider them.)

On back piece, copy only dots at top of mitten shapes. Cut out front and back felt pieces.

4. Trace and cut one of each green mitten, one grey chimney top, one white beard and two white mustache pieces (one piece reversed). Trace one pink face, but do not cut out until after it is embroidered in Step 4. Transfer design details to right side of felt.

5. Embroider front of stocking, using one strand of crewel yarn. Use grey yarn to chain-stitch all brick lines, working horizontal lines first. (See embroidery stitches in How-to Section.)

6. Pin the grey chimney top in place. Using grey yarn, blanket-stitch the long chimney edges between dots. (Short edges will be stitched when stocking front and back are joined.)

7. Complete sleeve trim, using white yarn to make straight stitches and French knots.

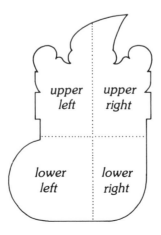

Figure 1 *Pattern sections joined to form stocking front.*

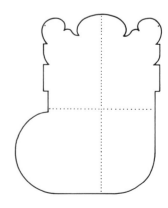

Figure 2 *For stocking back pattern, cut away Santa's hat.*

98

ACTUAL SIZE
pattern lines are
cutting lines for felt

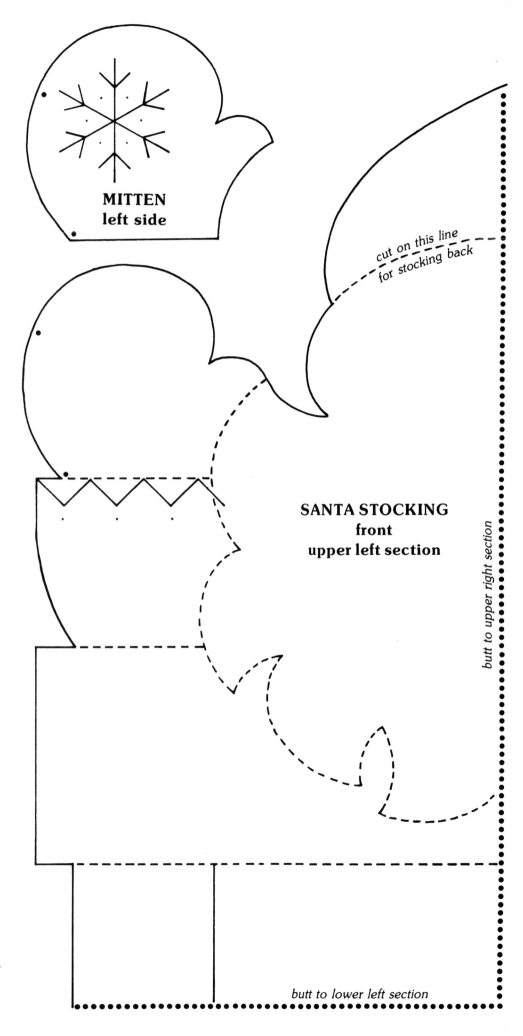

MITTEN
left side

SANTA STOCKING
front
upper left section

cut on this line
for stocking back

butt to upper right section

butt to lower left section

8. On the face, use grey yarn to backstitch eyes, and pink yarn to satin-stitch cheeks. Cut out face and baste in place behind beard, then join the two with white blanket stitches. Backstitch a red mouth on the beard. (It will be partially covered by the mustache.) Blanket-stitch edges of both mustache pieces, then tack them to face at nose area. Satin-stitch the red nose, letting stitches overlap mustache.

9. Pin completed head in position on stocking front, and edge with white blanket stitches. Push small amounts of stuffing between layers if you wish.

10. Pin mittens in place, butting them against beard. Use green yarn to blanket-stitch each mitten across the bottom and around thumb and mitten top, stitching between the dots. (Stitching on side of mitten will be completed later when stocking front and back are joined.)

11. Use red blanket stitches to finish top edge of stocking back (between dots on mitten shapes) and also to finish hat on stocking front. Use white straight stitches to make snowflakes, then add French knots between each segment.

12. Pin front and back together and join with blanket stitches; leave top open between dots on mittens. Use grey yarn around red chimney area and matching yarns around remaining parts.

13. Roll Santa's hat forward and tack with a fringe ball.

14. Tack plastic curtain ring to top center back of stocking.

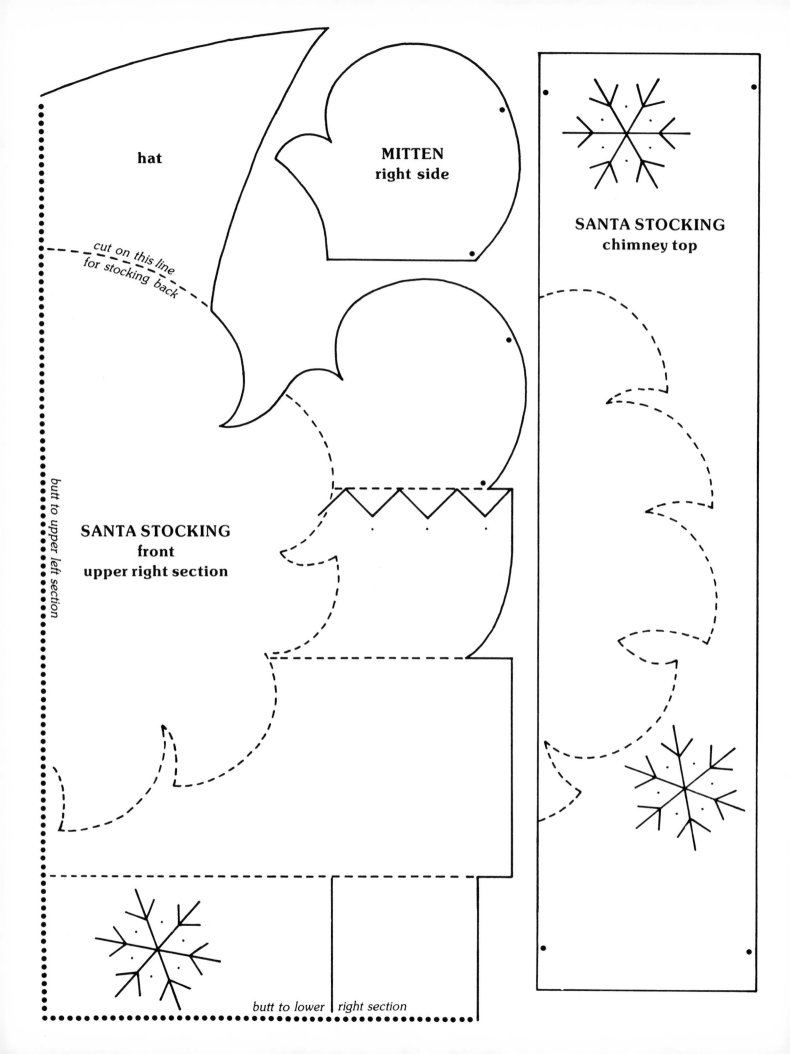

ACTUAL SIZE
pattern lines are cutting lines for felt

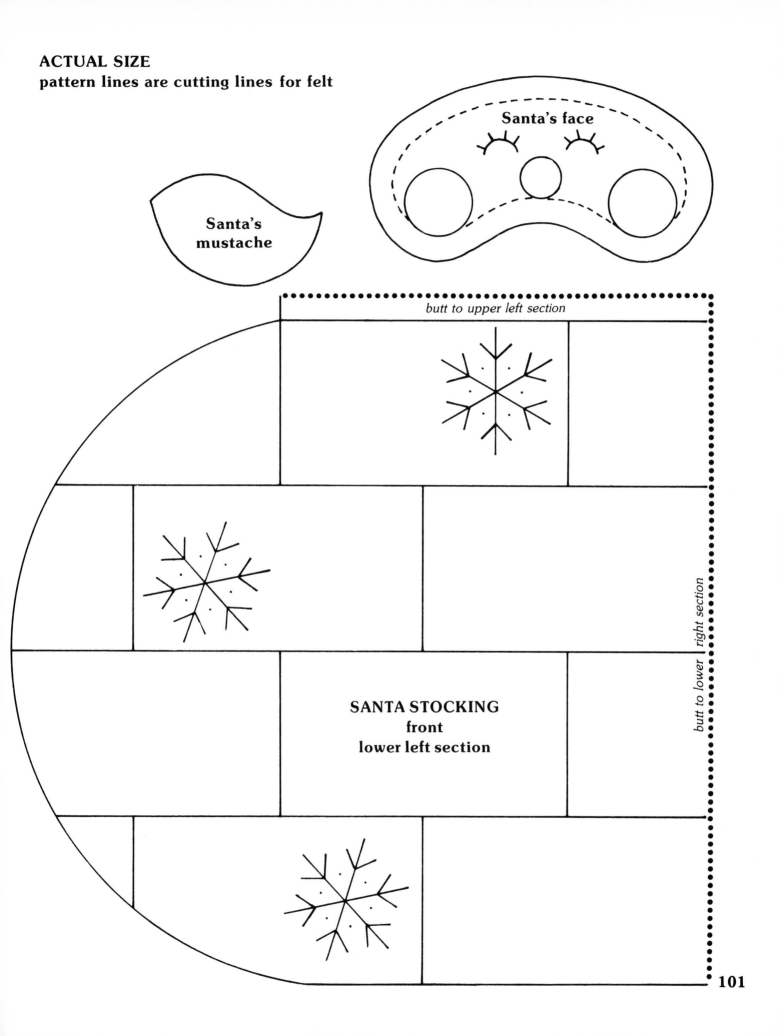

Santa's face

Santa's
mustache

butt to upper left section

butt to lower left right section

SANTA STOCKING
front
lower left section

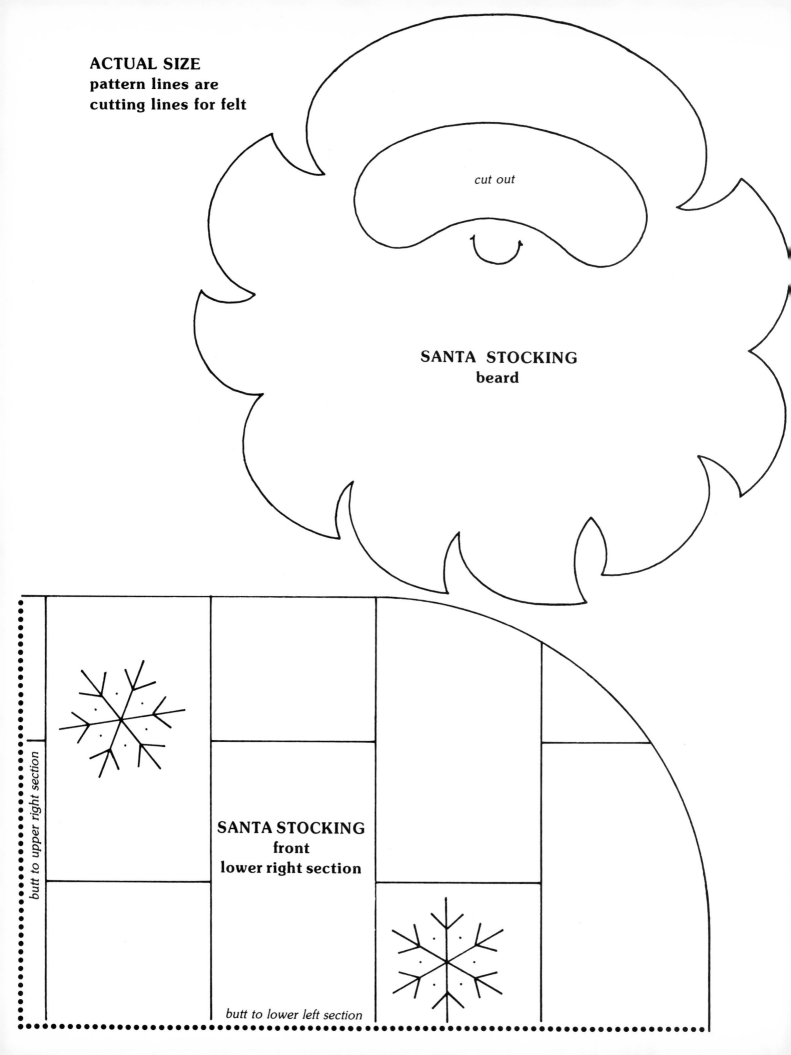

ACTUAL SIZE
pattern lines are
cutting lines for felt

cut out

SANTA STOCKING
beard

SANTA STOCKING
front
lower right section

butt to upper right section

butt to lower left section

Here's something you could hang in your home each year to officially open the holiday season. The banner is 52½x63" and contains 30 separate blocks. I sketched it years ago, but kept putting it at the bottom of the pile because drafting the patterns seemed too ambitious a project. You don't have to create the patterns, of course, but even so, making the banner is still a big job. I don't recommend it for beginners.

The banner is quilted, but that is optional. You could just tie each block at the corners.

Start early in the year. Promise yourself that you'll do a block every week, and you should be able to finish by Christmas! Or perhaps you could team up with family and friends to make the banner as a special gift for a December wedding.

On the other hand, instead of completing the design as a banner, you might make it into a unique quilt for a Christmas baby. Use just the central tree with a two-inch white border, so the finished baby quilt would measure approximately 35½x46". You could also use some single blocks for pillow tops.

The banner incorporates several traditional quilt squares, including Blazing Star (top row, center) and Four Stars (bottom row, center). Another is called Hens and Chickens (corner blocks), although the design looks like small trees when cut in green prints. The central section of the banner uses a motif called Pine Tree.

Noel Banner

(color photo, page 113)

Materials

3 yards white fabric, for backing and letters
1 yard blue with white dot fabric
Four different green and white prints, ³/₈ yard each, for trees
Brown with white print, 13x13", for tree trunks
Rainbow colored scraps:
  medium yellow, 13½x14½"
  yellow-orange, 11½x17
  orange, 17x35"
  red-orange, 11½x28"
  red, 9x11½"
  magenta, 9x11½"
  purple, 9x11½"
White background floral print, 8x24", for star blocks
Dark background floral print, 18x29", for letter blocks
Bright pink scrap, 17x22"
6¾ yards white wide bias tape
White thread
Polyester quilt batting, 55x66"
2 brass-finish café curtain rods, ⁵/₈" diameter, extending 48" to 86"

General Directions

The banner has 30 blocks, each 10½" square. Make the individual blocks, then sew them together.

Many patterns are repeated in different blocks, and some are used in reverse. Refer constantly

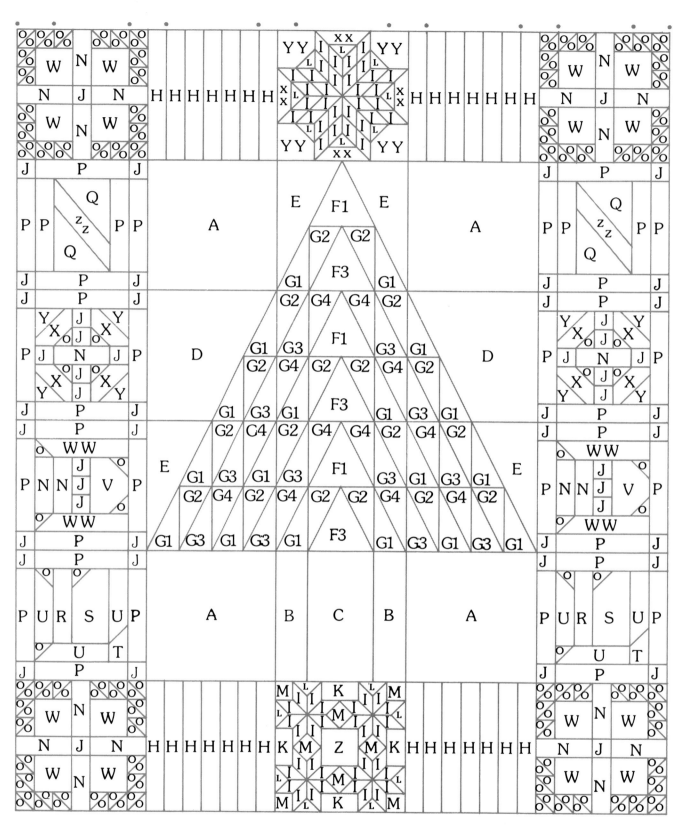

Figure 1 *Diagram of Noel Banner. Numbers (1-4) in central tree section indicate placement of the four different green and white prints.*

to Figure 1 as you cut and piece the banner. (If you don't, you're going to do a lot of ripping and recutting of fabric.)

Before starting work, cut a 9x36" strip from the white fabric (with the 36" side along the length); use this piece for the letter blocks. Save remainder for the backing.

1. Trace actual-size patterns E through ZZ; label and cut out. (Some patterns—F, G, H, I, J, M, O, P—will be used many times. To make them more durable, paste these pieces to cardboard and then cut out.)

2. Draw patterns A through C, as follows: A—$10\frac{1}{2}$x$10\frac{1}{2}$"; B—$2\frac{5}{8}$x$10\frac{1}{2}$"; C—$5\frac{1}{4}$x$10\frac{1}{2}$". Label and cut out.

3. To make pattern D, draw a $10\frac{1}{2}$" square. Fit pattern E inside the square (Figure 2), and trace the line from center of top edge to lower left corner. Label the larger section D, and cut out. *Pattern lines are stitching lines; add seam allowance when cutting fabric.*

4. To cut and stitch fabric, refer to directions for individual blocks following Step 13. Determine position of each pattern piece, then lay the pattern face down on wrong side of fabric. Trace and cut out, adding $\frac{1}{4}$" seam allowance on all sides. Arrange pieces to form each block

design before you begin stitching pieces, right sides together. Press seams as you go.

5. To assemble banner, lay all finished blocks in position, following Figure 1. Join blocks in horizontal rows, then join rows.

6. Measure banner; it should be 53x$63\frac{1}{2}$", including seam allowance. Note any differences, then cut backing to fit. Cut two pieces of white fabric, each 32x53" (or adjusted to fit your banner), and stitch together (on the 53" edges) with a $\frac{1}{4}$" seam.

7. Cut batting to fit banner. Stack and baste layers together in this order: backing, (wrong side up), batting, banner (right side up).

8. Hand quilt with white thread, following Figure 3.

9. To finish vertical edges, cut two lengths of white bias tape, each $63\frac{1}{2}$". Baste tape to edges of banner front, right sides together. Machine-stitch, fold tape to back, and hand-stitch tape flat to backing fabric.

10. To make hanging loops, cut 12 pieces of white fabric, each $3\frac{1}{4}$x$6\frac{1}{2}$". Fold each piece in half, right side inside, so short edges are together. Stitch a $\frac{1}{4}$" seam. Turn resulting tube right side out, position with seam at center back and press flat. To form loops, fold tube in half with seam inside and stitch raw edges together.

11. Lay loops on right side of banner along top and bottom edges; keep raw edges of loops even with raw edges of banner. Center loops on seams between blocks (see placement dots on Figure 1); keep end loops flush with banner edge. Baste in place.

12. To finish edges, cut two lengths of bias tape, each 54". Baste to top and bottom edges of banner front, right sides together. Machine-stitch, fold tape to back (enclosing raw edges of loops) and hand-stitch tape flat to backing fabric.

13. Insert rod through loops at top and bottom of banner.

Additional Directions
(for individual blocks)

First read Steps 1-4 under General Directions.

Corner blocks (directions for one block)

1. Use four patterns—J, O, N, W. From blue and white dot, cut 20 of the O, four N and one J. From each green print, cut four O and one W. From brown print, cut four O. Arrange pieces to form design, referring to color photo. (Do not mix the green prints—keep pieces of each print together.)

2. Start at upper left corner, and make a vertical strip by joining six O triangles (see Figure 4). From top down, place pieces in this order: blue dot, brown print, blue dot, green print, blue dot, green print. First stitch triangles to form squares, then join the squares.

Figure 2

Figure 3 *Quilting guide for Noel Banner. Quilt directly over seam lines as indicated.*

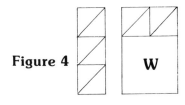

Figure 4

3. Next make a horizontal strip in this order: (from left) blue dot, green print, blue dot, green print. Stitch the horizontal strip to green print W; then join unit to vertical strip. Repeat to complete three more corner squares.

105

4. Use a blue dot N to join the two upper squares and the two lower squares (Figure 5). Make center strip by joining blue dot pieces N-J-N. Sew top and bottom sections to center strip.

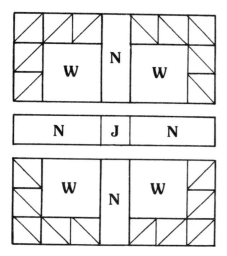

Figure 5 *Corner block*

5. Repeat to complete three more corner blocks. (Refer to color photo to check placement of green prints for each block.)

Rainbow blocks (directions for one block).

1. Use pattern H. Cut one H from each color: medium yellow, yellow-orange, orange, red-orange, red, magenta and purple.

2. Sew pieces together in order given above. (See Figure 1 and color photo.)

3. Repeat to complete three more rainbow blocks.

Blazing Star block (top row, center)

1. Use four patterns—I, L, XX, YY. From yellow (center of star), cut eight I. From yellow-orange (middle ring of star), cut 16 of I. From orange (star tips), cut eight I. From red-orange, cut eight L. From white floral, cut four XX and four YY. Arrange pieces to form design (see Figure 6 and color photo).

2. Work the blocks in sections. Join four I diamonds to make a star point (Figure 7), using one

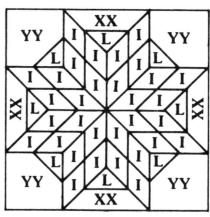

Figure 6 *Blazing Star block*

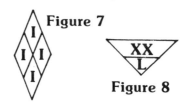

Figure 7

Figure 8

yellow, two yellow-orange (in middle) and one orange. Repeat to make seven more star points.

3. Join a red L triangle to each floral XX piece (Figure 8) to form four large triangles. Join a red L triangle to each floral YY piece (Figure 9) to form four large squares.

Figure 9

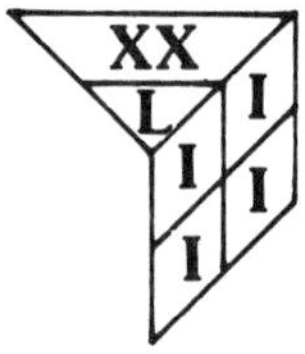

Figure 10

4. Stitch a large triangle to one edge of a star point (Figure 10); make four of these units. Stitch a square to one edge of each remaining star point (Figure 11) to make four of these units.

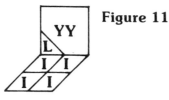

Figure 11

5. Stitch star point units together. Final seams are angled (shown as solid line in Figure 12), and should be done in two steps.
   Use small machine stitches. Begin at outside raw edge, stitch to pivot point (shown as dot),

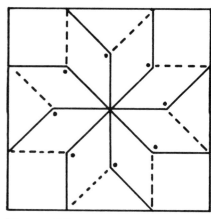

Figure 12

end stitching and secure thread. Begin again at pivot point and stitch to center of block. (Stitch only on seam lines; do not go into seam allowance at pivot point or center of block.)

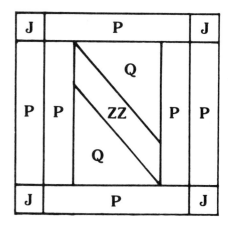

Figure 13 *Letter "N" block.*

Letter "N" block (directions for one block)

1. Use four patterns—J, P, Q, ZZ. From white, cut two P and one ZZ. From dark floral, cut two Q. From pink, cut four J. From orange, cut four P. Arrange pieces to form design (see Figure 13 and color photo).

2. Sew a floral Q to each side of white ZZ. Add a white P to each side of this unit, then add an orange P to top and bottom. Make two vertical strips by joining a pink J to each end of an orange P. Sew these strips to center unit to complete block.

3. Repeat steps to make a second "N" block.

106

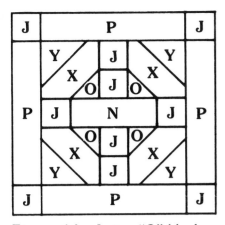

Figure 14 *Letter "O" block.*

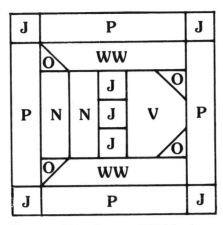

Figure 15 *Letter "E" block.*

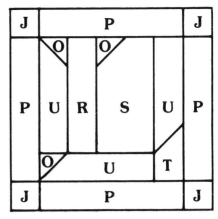

Figure 16 *Letter "L" block.*

Letter "O" block (directions for one block)

1. Use six patterns—J, N, O, P, X, Y. From white, cut four J and four X. From dark floral, cut two J, one N, four O and four Y. From pink, cut four P. From orange, cut four J. Arrange pieces to form design (see Figure 14 and color photo).

2. Join a floral Y and O to each side of a white X to make four squares. Add a white J to each floral J; use these units to join squares for top and bottom sections of letter.

3. Make a center horizontal strip by stitching a white J to each end of floral N. Use this strip to join top and bottom sections.

4. Stitch a pink P to top and bottom of letter. Then make two vertical strips by joining an orange J to each end of a pink P; stitch these strips to each side of letter.

5. Repeat steps to make another "O" block.

Letter "E" block (directions for one block)

1. Use six patterns—J, N, O, P, V, WW. From white, cut one J, two O, one N, one WW and one WW-reversed (flip the WW piece over and trace the reverse side). From dark floral, cut two J, one N, two O and one V. From pink, cut four J. From orange, cut four P. Arrange pieces to form design (see Figure 15 and color photo).

2. Make center vertical strip by stitching a floral J to top and bottom of the white J. Stitch a white O to each diagonal edge of floral V.

3. Piece center section by stitching floral N to white N. Add vertical J strip, then V unit.

4. Sew a floral O to the diagonal end of each white WW; add these strips to top and bottom of center section. Next add an orange P to each WW.

5. Stitch a pink J to each end of remaining orange P pieces; sew these units to sides of center section to complete block.

6. Repeat steps to make another "E" block.

Letter "L" block (directions for one block)

1. Use seven patterns—J, O, P, R, S, T, U. From white, cut two O, one R, one T and one U. From dark floral, cut one O, one S, one U and one U-reversed. From pink, cut four P. From orange, cut four J. Arrange pieces to form design (see Figure 16 and color photo).

2. Stitch a white O to diagonal edge of floral U piece. Stitch a floral O to diagonal edge of white U piece. Stitch a white O to diagonal edge of floral S. Stitch white T to diagonal edge of floral U-reversed.

3. To piece center section, join white O/floral U strip to white R; then add S/O unit.

4. Add floral O/white U strip to the bottom, then stitch T/U strip to the right side. Sew a pink P to top and bottom of center unit. Stitch an orange J to each end of remaining P pieces; add these strips to sides to complete block.

5. Repeat steps to make another "L" block.

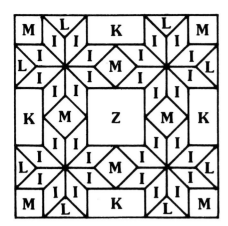

Figure 17 *Four Stars block.*

Four Stars block (bottom row, center)

1. Use five patterns—I, K, L, M, Z. From orange, cut one Z. From red-orange, cut 32 of I. From pink, cut four M. From white floral, cut four K, eight L and four M. Arrange pieces to form design (see Figure 17 and color photo).

2. Begin with upper left corner (Figure 18). Join red-orange diamonds in pairs, then stitch together to make a half star.

Figure 18

3. Add floral M to form a corner, and add a floral L to each side. (These angular seams must be done in two steps, as in the Blazing Star block.) Use small machine stitches, and stitch only on the seam line—do not go into seam allowance at beginning or end of seam. Complete four corner units.

4. To make each side (Figure 19), join red-orange diamonds in pairs, then stitch each pair to pink square M. Add a floral K. Make four of these side units.

108   **Figure 19**

5. Stitch the orange Z square to each side unit, and close the corner diagonal seams (joining diamonds). Add the four corner units to complete the block.

Center section (12 blocks including the large tree)

1. Use seven pattern pieces—A, B, C, D, E, F, G. To help arrange green print fabrics for large tree, give each of your prints a number, such as: 1-green dot; 2-candy stripe; 3-wallpaper stripe; 4-floral. Pieces on tree in Figure 1 are numbered as a placement guide.

2. From green print 1 (dot), cut three F, nine G and nine G-reversed. From green print 2 (candy stripe), cut nine G and nine G-reversed. From green print 3 (wallpaper stripe), cut three F, six G and six G-reversed. From green print 4 (floral), cut six G and six G-reversed.

3. From brown print, cut one C. From blue and white dot, cut four A, two B, one D, one D-reversed, two E and two E-reversed.

4. Work on one block at a time, and arrange pieces to form the design. When possible, join pieces to form rectangles or squares, then stitch these units together to form blocks.

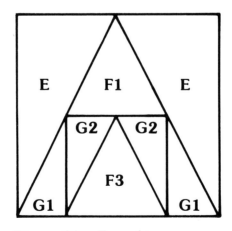

Figure 20 *Top of tree.*

5. Begin with top of tree (Figure 20). Join a G and G-reversed (print 2) to each side of F (print 3). Add an F (print 1) to the top, and a G and G-reversed (print 1) to each side. Sew this unit to blue dot E pieces.

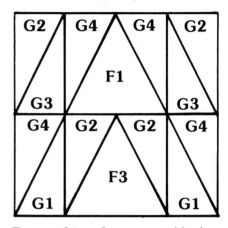

Figure 21 *Center tree block.*

6. Make two center tree blocks (Figure 21). First join adjacent triangles to make rectangles and squares. Stitch these units together to make horizontal rows, then join the two rows to complete block.

7. Follow Figure 1 to piece remaining center blocks for sides of tree and tree trunk.

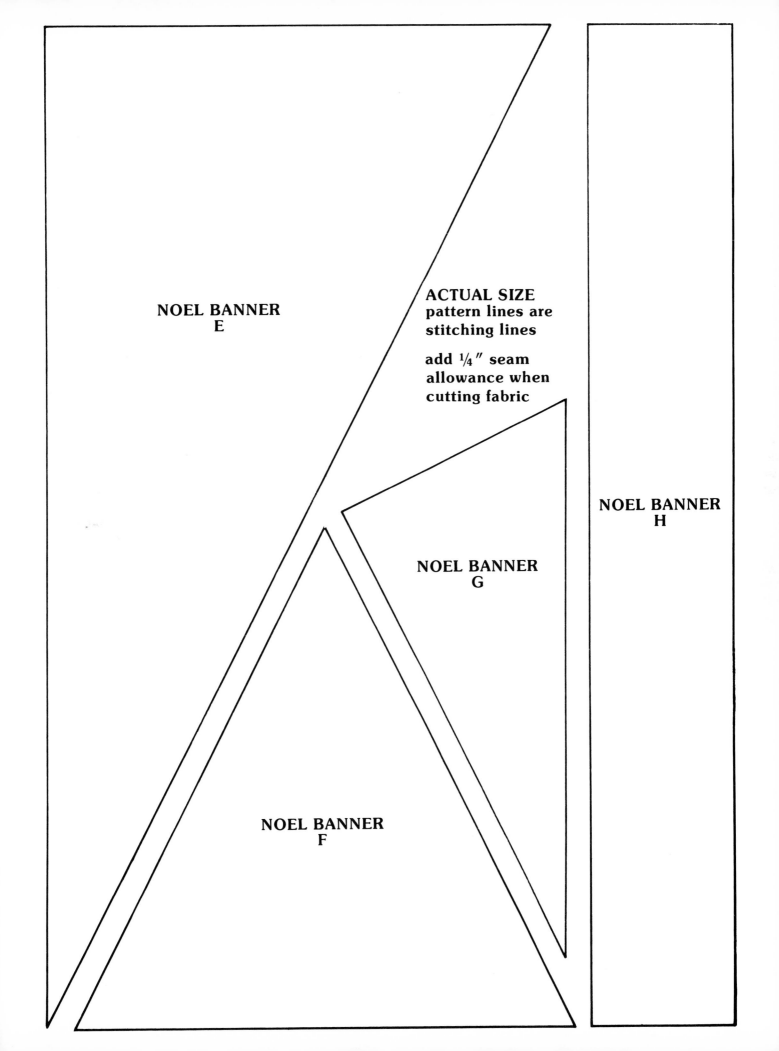

**NOEL BANNER
E**

ACTUAL SIZE
pattern lines are
stitching lines

add ¼ ″ seam
allowance when
cutting fabric

**NOEL BANNER
G**

**NOEL BANNER
H**

**NOEL BANNER
F**

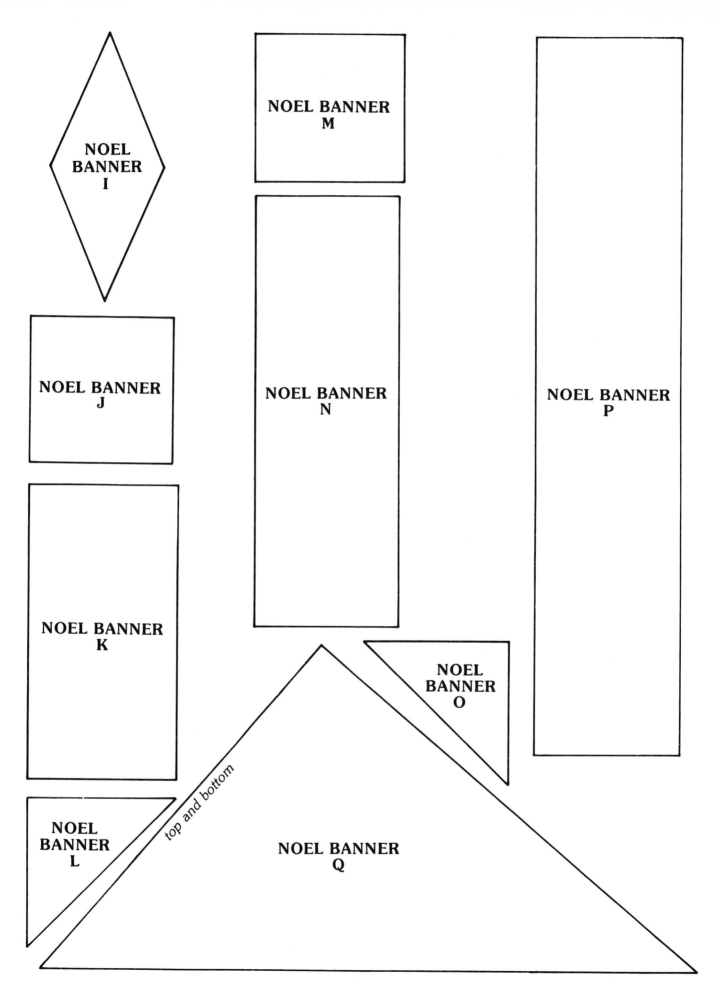

NOEL BANNER
I

NOEL BANNER
M

NOEL BANNER
P

NOEL BANNER
J

NOEL BANNER
N

NOEL BANNER
K

NOEL
BANNER
O

NOEL
BANNER
L

top and bottom

NOEL BANNER
Q

110

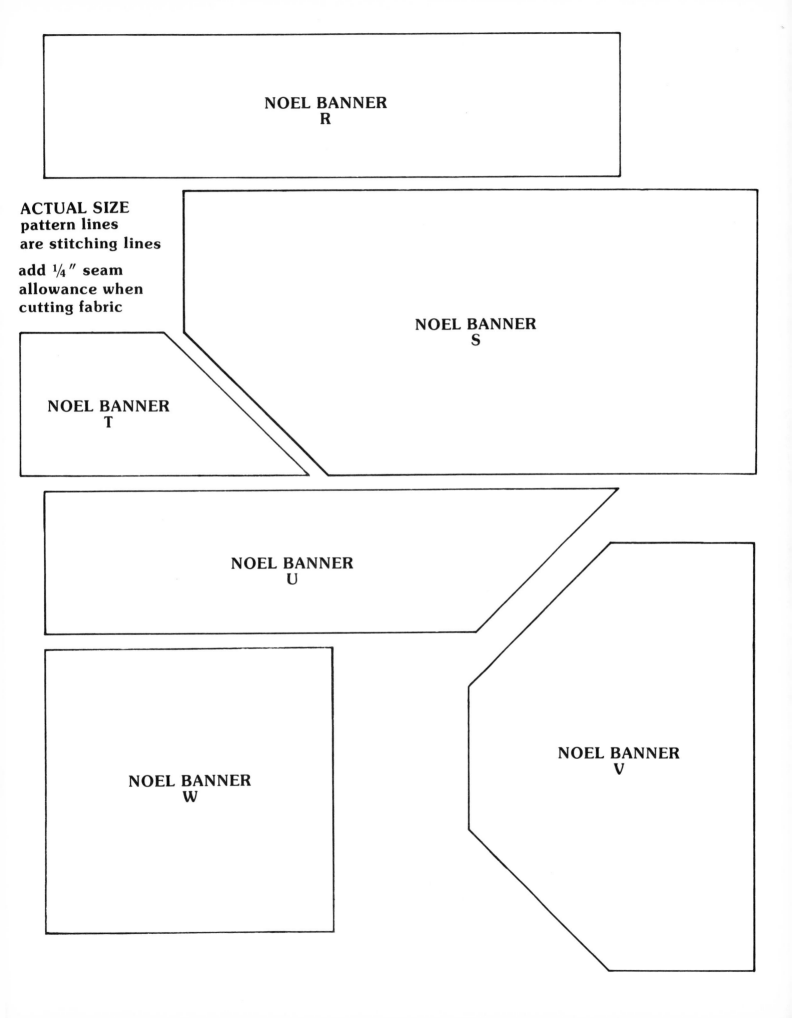

NOEL BANNER
R

ACTUAL SIZE
pattern lines
are stitching lines

add ¼″ seam
allowance when
cutting fabric

NOEL BANNER
S

NOEL BANNER
T

NOEL BANNER
U

NOEL BANNER
W

NOEL BANNER
V

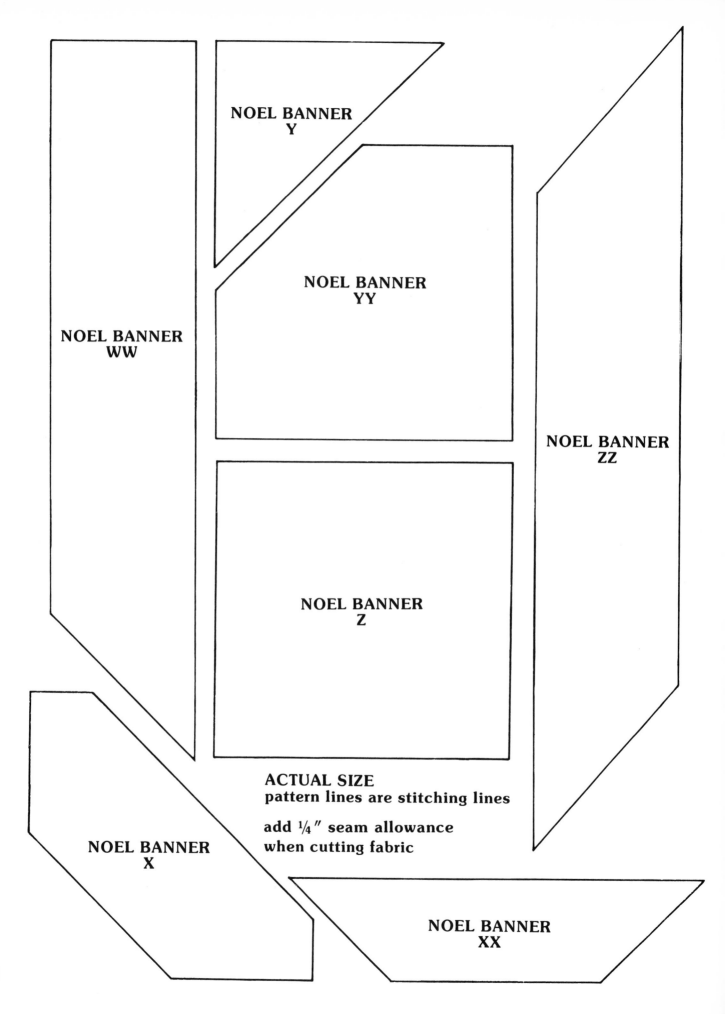

NOEL BANNER
Y

NOEL BANNER
YY

NOEL BANNER
WW

NOEL BANNER
ZZ

NOEL BANNER
Z

ACTUAL SIZE
pattern lines are stitching lines

add ¼″ seam allowance
when cutting fabric

NOEL BANNER
X

NOEL BANNER
XX

Hang this Noel Banner each year to officially open the holiday season (see page 103).

114

Make this Christmas Tote Bag as a gift—or keep it yourself for delivering smaller gifts. Color-coordinated tree ornaments include quilt squares, cross-stitch designs and a small basket woven from ribbons (see page 122).

Santa Stocking decorates
the fireplace until Santa himself
arrives to fill the stocking
with goodies (see page 98).

116

Hang one of these wreaths on the wall and use one to circle a candle on your Christmas table. The wreaths are about 12" across, and they're backed with embroidery hoops or circles of cardboard.

I used tiny blanket stitches to embroider the felt edges. If you want to make a speedier version, substitute running stitches—or even machine stitches.

Directions tell you how to make the wreaths, but you can make individual ornaments, if you wish. The angels are self-contained, so you can cut pattern pieces for just one. For a single Santa, trace one unit from the wreath pattern, then use the angel hand pattern to cut two hands from pink felt. Trim Santa's sleeves with white felt.

Angel and Santa Wreaths

Angel Wreath

Materials

White felt, 12x20"
Light pink felt, 3½x4½"
Black felt, 4½x5¼"
Tan felt, 4½x9"
Brown felt, 4½x9"
Fabric scraps, 4½x9" each: red floral, red stripe, red check, green floral, green stripe, green check
1½ yards narrow shirred white lace
White thread
Embroidery thread, 1 skein each: white, light pink, medium pink, tan, brown, black, red, green
Fusible web, 4x4" (or rubber cement)
2 embroidery hoops, 4" and 8" diameter (or cardboard, 9x9")
Polyester stuffing
White glue

Directions

You'll need a compass to help draw the backing pattern.

1. Draw an 11" circle on tracing paper and fold in half. Trace backing pattern onto each half of circle to make complete backing pattern (see Figure 1).

2. Trace single halo/wing pattern, adding center placement dot and dots for leaf embroidery. Trace patterns for body, hair, face and hand. Cut out all patterns; use tape to reinforce back-

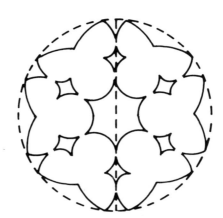

Figure 1   Guide for making complete backing pattern.

ing pattern where halos and wings join. Make template of face pattern by cutting out eyes, cheeks, nose and mouth lines.

Pattern line for body is stitching line; add seam allowance when cutting fabric. All other pattern lines are cutting lines for felt.

3. On white felt, trace one full backing piece and six single halo/wing pieces. Transfer all dots (see transfer directions in How-to Section). Cut out pieces.

4. Use two strands of embroidery thread for all embroidery unless otherwise noted, and see directions for stitches in How-to Section. With green thread, make lazy-daisy stitch (leaves) on each halo/wing piece, using dots as guides. With red thread, make

French knots (berries) between the leaves.

5. Lightly glue each halo/wing piece to backing, and blanket-stitch around edges with white thread. Set piece aside.

6. For hands, cut two 2x2" pieces from pink, from tan and from brown felt. Make a double layer of each color, using fusible web or rubber cement. Trace and cut out four hands from each color. Edge with blanket stitches in matching thread.

7. For faces, work with single layers of pink, tan and brown felt, and trace two faces on each color. Use template to transfer design lines to right side of felt. Satin-stitch medium pink cheeks and black eyes. Backstitch smiles (with single strand of thread), using red thread on pink and tan faces, and medium pink thread on brown faces. Use one straight stitch for each nose with thread to match felt. Cut out faces.

8. On single layers of tan, brown and black felt, trace one each of curly hair front and back patterns, and one each of straight hair front and back patterns. Cut out (a total of six sets of hair). Clip hair fronts at each side along bangs to dotted lines.

9. Add hair fronts to faces, combining tan hair with pink faces, brown hair with tan faces,

117

Figure 2 *Assembly guide for angels.*

and black hair with brown faces. (Faces tuck under hair at top and overlap hair at sides.) Lightly glue faces in place. With embroidery thread to match hair, blanket-stitch bangs to faces.

10. To make bodies, fold each print scrap, right sides together. Trace body pattern on wrong side, transferring placement dots to fabric. Before cutting, machine-stitch each outline, leaving end of sleeves and bottom of skirt open. Cut out, adding 1/8" seam allowance. Clip into V areas at neck and under arms; clip corners of skirt. Turn right side out.

11. For each body, turn under skirt and sleeve hems. Finger press and baste, keeping areas open. Cut two 2¼" pieces of shirred lace, and hand-stitch entirely around sleeve edges. Insert correct color hand (see color photo) and close opening.

12. Cut a 3⅛" piece of shirred lace for skirt bottom and hand-stitch to one side. Stuff body lightly, keeping figure flat; close opening with invisible hand stitches.

13. Satin-stitch red buttons on green print bodies and green buttons on red print bodies.

14. Refer to color photo and Figure 2 for assembling angels. Lightly glue each felt head front to a body, lining up bottom edge of face with placement dot on body. Cut a 1¾" piece of shirred lace, insert under chin and baste in place.

15. Glue hair back to back of head. With embroidery thread to match hair, blanket-stitch around edge of hair to join front and back pieces.

With thread to match face, blanket-stitch around edge of face. Make invisible straight stitches to catch lower edge of face to back of head, pulling thread tightly to define neck.

16. Pin each angel to a halo/wing on backing, matching placement dots. Stretch hands gently to meet, if necessary. Tack angels in place at back of heads and sleeve edges.

17. Sew one ring of the 8" embroidery hoop to back of wreath, tacking to center back of each angel and also where wings touch. Sew one ring of the 4" hoop to back of wreath, tacking where halos touch. (If you use cardboard, cut ½"-wide rings to substitute for embroidery hoops.)

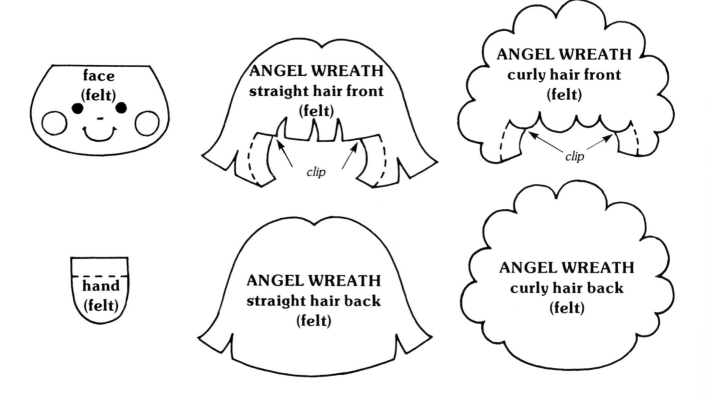

118

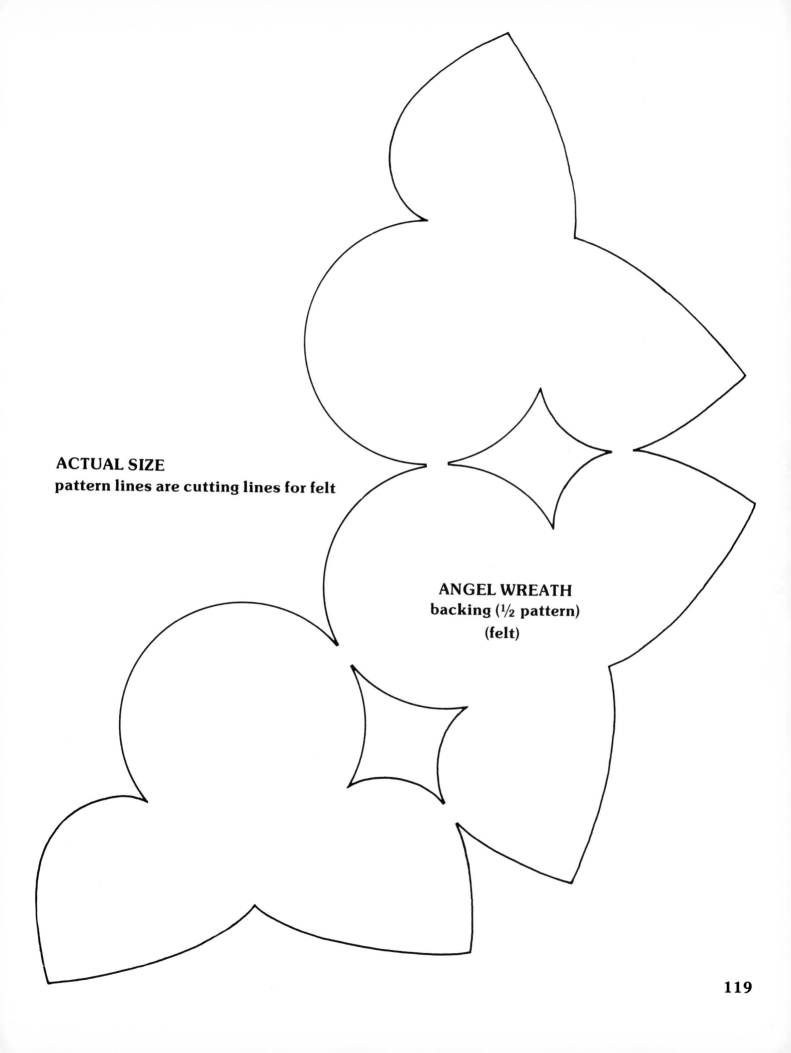

ACTUAL SIZE
pattern lines are cutting lines for felt

ANGEL WREATH
backing (½ pattern)
(felt)

119

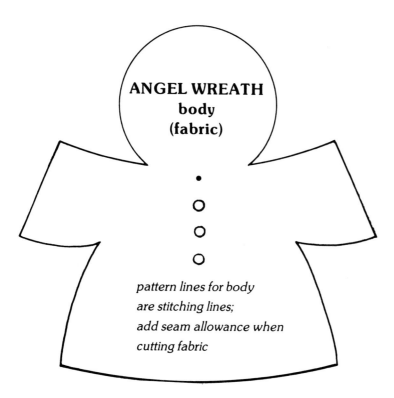

ANGEL WREATH
body
(fabric)

*pattern lines for body
are stitching lines;
add seam allowance when
cutting fabric*

ACTUAL SIZE
**pattern lines are stitching lines for fabric,
and cutting lines for felt**

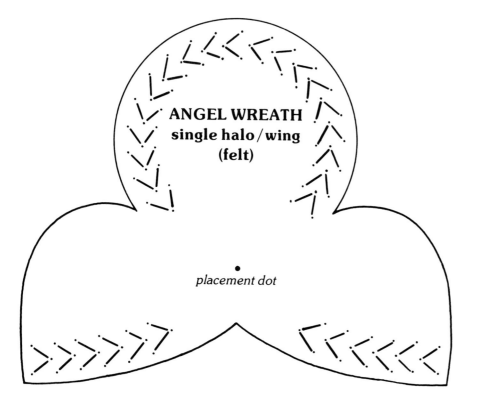

ANGEL WREATH
single halo / wing
(felt)

placement dot

Santa Wreath

Materials

Red felt, 13x25″
Light pink felt, 4x5″
White felt, 8½x11″
Green felt, 6x6″
Embroidery thread, 1 skein each:
  red, black, green, medium pink
Polyester stuffing
8 white small fringe balls,
  ½″ diameter
Embroidery hoop, 7″ diameter (or
  cardboard, 8x8″)
White glue

Directions

You'll need a compass to help
draw the wreath pattern.

1. Draw a 12″ circle on tracing paper, and fold into quarters.
Trace pattern for front and backing (two Santas) from book onto
each quarter circle to make a
complete wreath pattern (see
Figure 1); do not copy the
design lines.

2. Trace patterns for face,
beard/hatband, coat band and

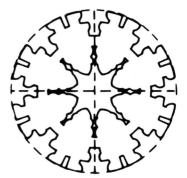

Figure 1 *Guide for making
complete front and backing pattern.*

boot. Cut out patterns. Make
template of face pattern by cutting out eyes, nose and cheeks.
*Pattern lines are cutting lines
for felt.*

3. On red felt, trace around
wreath pattern twice to make
one front and one backing piece.
Cut out backing only.

4. From pink felt, trace and
cut out eight faces; use template
to mark design lines on right
side. From white felt, trace and

cut out eight beard/hatband pieces and eight coat band pieces. From green felt, trace and cut out eight boots; then flip boot pattern over to trace and cut out eight reversed boots.

5. Glue a beard/hatband piece over each face and let dry. Position these units on uncut wreath front; glue in place and let dry.

6. Embroider faces, using two strands of embroidery thread; refer to How-to Section for stitches. With white embroidery thread, blanket-stitch around face, and where hatband and beard overlap red suit.

Satin-stitch black eyes, pink cheeks and red nose. (Nose overlaps beard.) Backstitch red mouth.

7. Cut out wreath front. Glue boots to wreath front. Glue coat bands in place, overlapping boot tops, and let dry. With white embroidery thread, blanket-stitch coat band where it overlaps red suit and green boots.

8. Pin wreath front to backing. Use two strands of matching threads and blanket stitches to join layers at Santa's arms and entire lower body (leave only head open). Stuff lightly, pushing batting into boots, arms and body with blunt end of crochet hook. Close the head area with blanket stitches and matching threads.

9. Stitch a fringe ball to the top of each hat.

10. Sew one ring of embroidery hoop to back of wreath, tacking to Santa's arms. (If you use cardboard, cut a ½"-wide ring to substitute for embroidery hoop.)

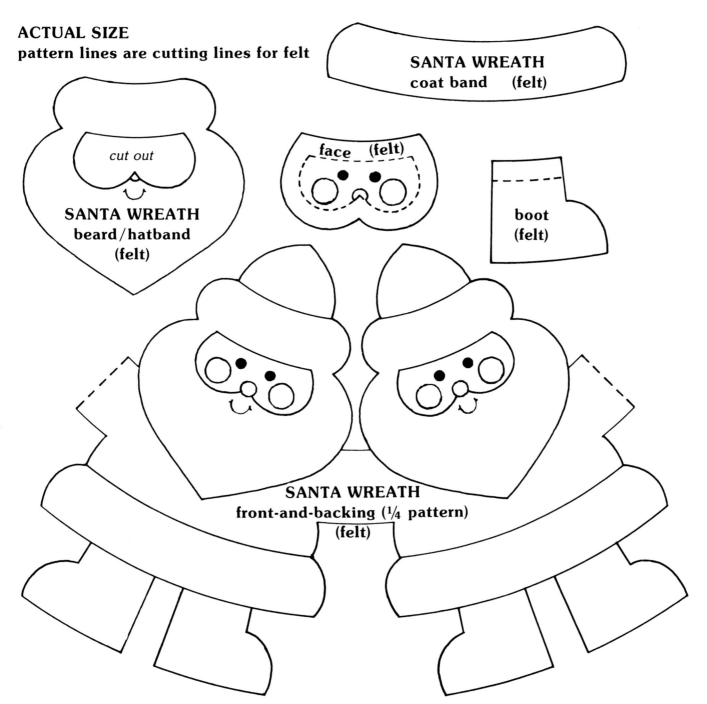

ACTUAL SIZE
pattern lines are cutting lines for felt

SANTA WREATH
coat band   (felt)

cut out

SANTA WREATH
beard/hatband
(felt)

face   (felt)

boot
(felt)

SANTA WREATH
front-and-backing (¼ pattern)
(felt)

Pink and green can be a lovely color combination for the Christmas season, and some years these colors seem just right to me. Here, I've used pink and green for a Christmas tote bag and a whole group of fabric and ribbon ornaments. I wanted everything to be soft—to look at and to touch.

My inspiration for the tote bag came from an old quilt block pattern that my grandmother used over 50 years ago. Designs for the ornaments use old crafts, too—patchwork, cross-stitch embroidery and ribbon weaving.

If you make the tote bag first, you can carry the rest of your work around in it.

Christmas Tote Bag & Ornaments

(color photo, page 114)

Christmas Tote Bag

Materials

White fabric such as piqué, 21x42″
Pink fabric, 10x16″
Green print, 4½x22″
Second green print, 3½x6½″
Brown print or dot, 2x3½″
Pink print or check, 19x36″, for lining
Thread to match or blend with fabrics
Polyester quilt batting, 21x38″
Non-woven interfacing (medium weight), 19x36″ (optional)

Directions

1. Trace actual-size patterns A through J onto tracing paper, label and cut out. *Pattern lines are stitching lines; add seam allowance when cutting fabric.*

2. To make patchwork block (Figure 1), trace pattern pieces on wrong side of fabric; cut out, adding ¼″ seam allowance.

From white, cut two E pieces, three G and three G-reversed pieces (flip the G pattern over and trace reverse side), one H and one H-reversed.

From green print, cut four A, two B, and two C pieces. From second green print, cut one F.

From brown print, cut one D. From pink, cut one I, one I-reversed and two J pieces.

3. To assemble block, arrange pieces right side up, following Figure 1. Work with one side of tree, and press seams flat. Sew A to H (right sides together), B to G, A to G and C to G. Join these four strips. Repeat to make reverse side of tree.

Add a pink I to each side, then join the two sides.

Sew the two E pieces to D; add F to complete a square. Sew square to upper tree section. Add two pink J pieces to complete block.

4. Cut a piece of batting 13¾″ square. Lay on wrong side of patchwork block, with top edge along hem line of bag. Lightly tack batting to hem line, catching only one thread with each stitch. Quilt by hand around large center square, tree trunk, branches and ground line.

5. Cut bag back (with sides and bottom) from white fabric, following dimensions in Figure 2; add ¼″ seam allowance to all edges. Transfer lines for top hem, side and bottom edges to right side of fabric with bastings. (See transfer directions in How-to Section.)

6. Cut batting to fit back, omitting top hem. Lay batting on wrong side of fabric along top hem line and tack, as in Step 4. Baste layers together, sewing directly over bastings on side and

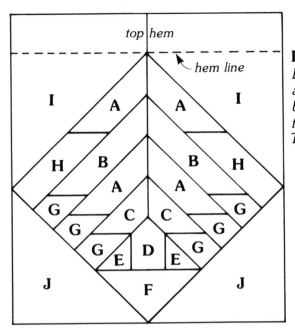

Figure 1
Bag front and quilt block guide for Christmas Tote Bag.

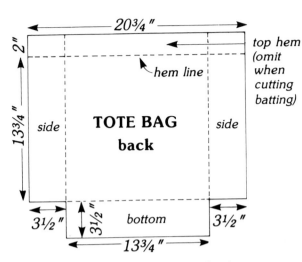

Figure 2 *Guide for drawing back pattern; seam allowance is not included.*

Figure 3 *Guide for drawing lining patterns; seam allowance is not included.*

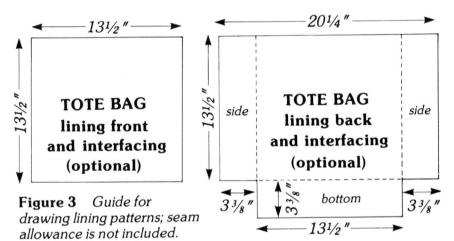

Figure 4 *Guide for making handle; seam allowance is included.*

bottom edges. (This holds batting in place when you box the edges later.) Also baste along raw edges.

7. Right sides together, pin and stitch back and front pieces, first along sides, then long bottom seam, then short bottom seams. Trim batting close to seams and press seams flat as you work. Clip off corners.

8. Turn bag right side out and push out corners around base. Press creases along all edges at sides and bottom.

9. To box the edges, place pins perpendicular to creases. Topstitch very close to edge by machine, first the sides, then long bottom edges, then short bottom edges.

10. Cut two pink lining pieces,

following dimensions on pattern diagrams in Figure 3; add 1/4" seam allowance to all edges except top. Transfer lines to right side of fabric with bastings.

11. Cut interfacing, if desired, following same dimensions; baste to wrong side of lining.

12. Right sides together, pin and stitch lining front to back, first along the sides, then long bottom edge, then short bottom edges. Press seams as you work.

13. To box lining, press and stitch (on wrong side) along all edges without seams. Leave lining wrong side out, and push into bag. Match corners, and fold top of bag over lining at hem line. Turn under raw edge on bag; pin, hand-stitch to lining.

14. To make handles, cut two

white pieces, each 5x17" (see Figure 4). Seam allowance is included on these pieces. Cut two batting strips 1 1/2 x17".

15. Fold each fabric handle piece in half lengthwise, right side out, and press. Open fabric, lay one edge of batting strip along center line, and tack batting to fold line. Fold raw edges of fabric to center fold line (covering batting). Then refold handle down center, and pin outside edges together. Baste both long sides, and topstitch close to edge. Remove bastings.

16. Pin a handle in place on front and back of bag, with ends about 4" from sides. Turn raw edges of handle under 1/2", and keep turned edges even with top of bag lining. Hand-stitch handle to bag.

123

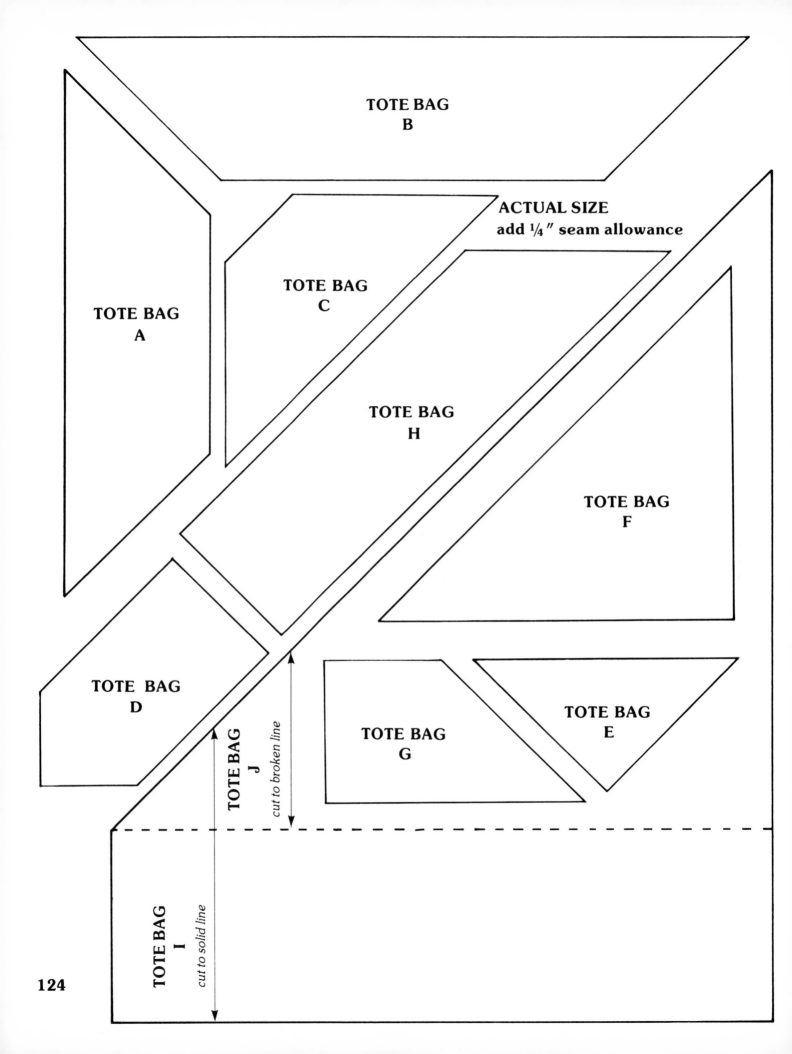

TOTE BAG
B

ACTUAL SIZE
add ¼″ seam allowance

TOTE BAG
C

TOTE BAG
A

TOTE BAG
H

TOTE BAG
F

TOTE BAG
D

TOTE BAG
J
cut to broken line

TOTE BAG
G

TOTE BAG
E

TOTE BAG
I
cut to solid line

124

Quilt Squares

General Materials
(for each ornament)

13¾″ white eyelet ruffle (1″ wide)
Polyester stuffing
13¾″ grosgrain ribbon in brilliant pink, medium green or dark green, ¼″ or ⅜″ wide

General Directions

1. Copy and label actual-size patterns on tracing paper and cut out. *All pattern lines are stitching lines; add seam allowance when cutting fabric.*

2. Trace pattern outlines face down on wrong side of fabric. Cut out, adding ¼″ seam allowance. Pin or baste pieces together before stitching, making sure corners match exactly. (Refer to directions under individual ornaments for piecing sequence.) Press seams flat as you go.

3. Pin eyelet ruffle to edge of finished square, right sides together. (Scalloped edge of eyelet will be toward center.) Fold ruffle binding at corners so ruffle will be extra full there; pin fullness out of way. Baste on seam line.

4. Pin back to front, right sides together, with ruffle in between. Stitch around edge, leaving 1″ open for turning. Turn to right side, stuff lightly and keep flat; close opening by hand.

5. For hanging loop, cut 4½″ strip of ribbon and fold each end under ¼″. Form loop by stitching folded edges together with invisible stitches; also stitch up ¼″ along each side from fold to hold cut edges in place. Attach loop seam to one corner of ornament behind ruffle.

6. To make bow, cut ribbon 3½″ long. Overlap ends ¼″ to form a loop, then tack ends at center of ribbon to make a bow. Cut a piece of ribbon 4¾″ long for streamers; attach under bow at center. Wrap center of bow with a 1″ length of ribbon to hide stitches; overlap at back and tack. Sew bow to top of hanging loop.

Twin Sisters

First check list of General Materials for all ornaments.

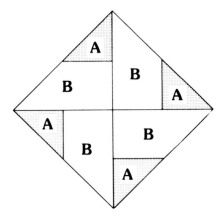

Figure 1   *Twin Sisters.*

Additional Materials

Green print scrap, 3x4½″
Pink print scrap, 3½x7″
Pink or green print scrap, 3½x3½″, for back
Thread to match

Directions

1. Follow Steps 1-2 under General Directions. Cut four green print A triangles and four pink print B shapes.

2. To piece block, refer to Figure 1, and sew each green A piece to an adjoining pink B piece, right sides together, to make four triangles. Sew triangles together in pairs to form two larger triangles. Join the two triangles to complete square.

3. Finish ornament, following Steps 3-6 under General Directions. Use pink ribbon for hanging loop and bow.

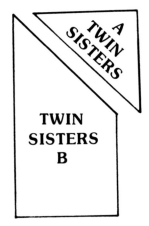

Economy

First check list of General Materials for all ornaments.

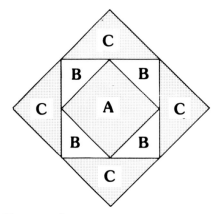

Figure 2   *Economy.*

Additional Materials

Light pink print scrap, 2x2″
Bright pink print scrap, 1¾x7″
Green print scrap, 2x8½″
Pink or green print scrap, 3½x3½″, for back
Thread to match

Directions

1. Follow Steps 1-2 under General Directions. Cut one light pink A square. Cut four bright pink B triangles. Cut four green C triangles.

2. To piece block, refer to Figure 2. Sew a bright pink triangle to each side of light pink A square to create a larger square. Sew a green C triangle to each side of the new square to complete design.

3. Finish ornament, following Steps 3-6 under General Directions. Use medium green ribbon for hanging loop and bow.

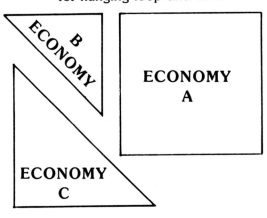

Shoofly

First check list of General Materials for all ornaments.

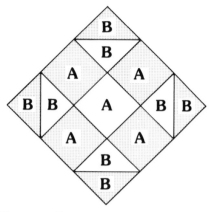

Figure 3 *Shoofly.*

Additional Materials

White with pink print scrap, 2¾x6″
Green print scrap, 3½x7½″
Pink or green print scrap, 3½x3½″, for back
Thread to match

Directions

1. Follow Steps 1-2 under General Directions. From white with pink print, cut one A square and four B triangles. From green print, cut four A squares and four B triangles.

2. To piece block, refer to Figure 3. Sew a green B triangle to each print B triangle to make four corner squares.

Make an outside row by sewing a corner square to each side of a green A square. Repeat to make another outside row.

Make a middle row by sewing a green A square to each side of the print A square. Join the three rows to complete design.

3. Finish ornament, following Steps 3-6 under General Directions. Use pink ribbon for hanging loop and bow.

Snowflake

First check list of General Materials for all ornaments.

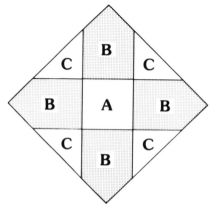

Figure 4 *Snowflake.*

Additional Materials

White fabric scrap, 1¾x1¾″
Bright green print scrap, 2½x6¾″
Bright pink print scrap, 1½x6¾″
Pink or green print scrap, 3½x3½″, for back
Thread to match

Directions

1. Follow Steps 1-2 under General Directions. From white fabric, cut one A square. From green print, cut four B pieces. From pink print, cut four C triangles.

2. To piece block, refer to Figure 4. Sew two pink C triangles to a green B piece to form a larger triangle. Repeat to complete a second large triangle.

Sew a green B to opposite sides of the white A square to form a middle strip. Join triangles to middle strip to complete square.

3. Finish ornament, following Steps 3-6 under General Directions. Use dark green ribbon for hanging loop and bow.

SNOW-FLAKE A

SNOWFLAKE B

C SNOWFLAKE

SHOOFLY A

SHOOFLY B

Cross-Stitch Ornaments

Materials
(for each ornament)

Pink or light green gingham scrap
  (¹/₈" check), 6x6"
White batiste, 6x6"; white thread
Print scrap, 4x4", for back
11" white eyelet ruffle, 1" wide
Polyester stuffing
Embroidery thread (see diagram of
  individual design for colors)
13¾" grosgrain ribbon in brilliant
  pink, medium green or dark green,
  ¼" or ³/₈" wide

Directions

Each square on diagram equals one square on gingham. For embroidery, make diagonal cross stitches, letting each cross stitch fill one gingham square.

1. Draw a 3" circle on cardboard; cut out. *Pattern line is stitching line; add seam allowance when cutting fabric.*

2. Trace circle on batiste, and baste batiste to wrong side of gingham on circle line. Refer to individual diagram for colors of gingham and embroidery thread. Center design. Use two strands of thread, and complete cross-stitch design.

3. Cut out circle, adding ¼"

seam allowance. Baste edge of eyelet ruffle to edge of gingham, right sides together. (Scalloped edge of ruffle will be toward center of circle.)

4. Trace around circle pattern on wrong side of print scrap for back; cut out, adding ¼" seam allowance. Pin ornament front to back, right sides together with ruffle in between. Machine-stitch around outside, leaving 1" open for turning. Clip curve.

5. Turn right side out, stuff lightly and keep flat. Close opening by hand.

6. To make hanging loop with bow, see Steps 5-6 under General Directions for Quilt Square Ornaments, page 125.

Color key:

◩ *brown*

▦ *medium green*

⊡ *medium pink*

☒ *dark green*

▯ *yellow*

△ *deep pink*

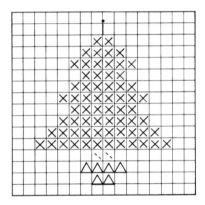

CROSS-STITCH TREE
Use green gingham. Add green straight stitch and yellow French knot at top of tree. Use pink ribbon for loop and bow.

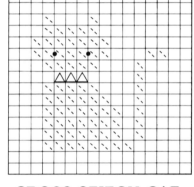

CROSS-STITCH CAT
Use pink gingham. Add green French knots for eyes. Use medium green ribbon for loop and bow.

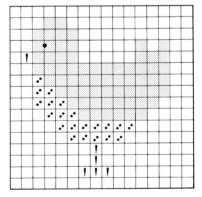

CROSS-STITCH BIRD
Use green gingham. Add brown French knot for eye. Use dark green ribbon for loop and bow.

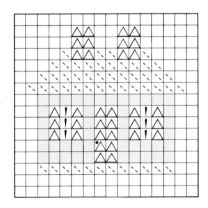

CROSS-STITCH HOUSE
Use pink gingham. Add brown French knot for doorknob. Use pink ribbon for loop and bow.

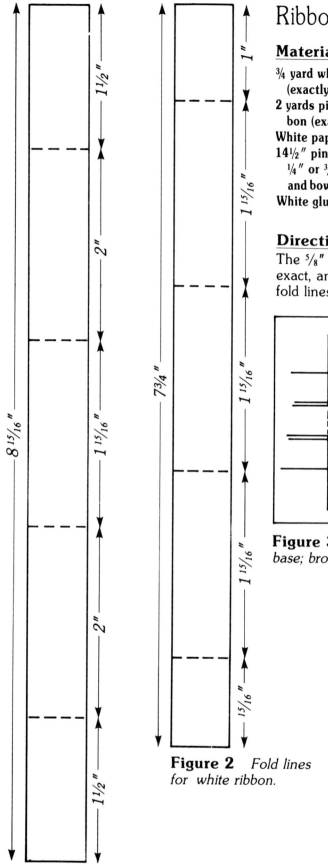

Figure 1 *Fold lines for colored ribbon.*

Figure 2 *Fold lines for white ribbon.*

Ribbon Basket

Materials

¾ yard white grosgrain ribbon (exactly ⅝″ wide)
2 yards pink or green grosgrain ribbon (exactly ⅝″ wide)
White paper, for backing
14½″ pink or green grosgrain ribbon, ¼″ or ⅜″ wide, for hanging loop and bow
White glue (or rubber cement)

Directions

The ⅝″ ribbon width should be exact, and measurements for fold lines should be accurate.

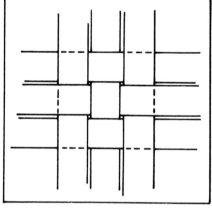

Figure 3 *Weaving the square base; broken lines are fold lines.*

1. Cut pink or green ⅝″ ribbon into six lengths, each 8¹⁵⁄₁₆″ long. (Remaining ribbon piece is for handle.) Cut six backing strips of paper to same size, and copy marks for fold lines (on paper strips) from Figure 1.

Cut white ⅝″ ribbon into three lengths, each 7¾″ long. Cut three backing strips of paper to the same size, and copy marks for fold lines (on paper) from Figure 2.

2. Glue ribbon to same-size white paper strips (fold marks out), using rubber cement or white glue. (If you use rubber cement, spread cement on each surface, let dry, then press surfaces together. If you use white glue, spread glue evenly on paper and immediately press ribbon against it; then place layered strip between clean papers under heavy book to dry.)

When strips are dry, fold each, ribbon side out, on fold lines.

3. To weave basket, begin with the six colored ribbons. Refer to Figure 3, and tightly weave a square base. Use tape on the paper side to secure.

Fold ends of ribbon up (on broken lines) for sides. Use white ribbon to weave sides, and hide ribbon ends at start and finish behind a colored strip. Use tape to secure strips as you work.

4. To make handle, cut two strips ⅝″ ribbon, each 6½″ long. Cut a strip of paper to same size, and glue between ribbon strips. Curl layered strip over edge of table while damp.

Apply glue to each end of handle (both sides) and push ends into pockets formed by weaving at top of basket.

5. To make a hanging loop, cut a strip of ⅜″ ribbon 5¾″ long. Form a loop, with handle inside, and sew ends together. Add ribbon bow, following Step 6 under General Directions for Square Quilt Ornaments, page 125. (Bow can be attached to basket, omitting hanging loop.) Fill with tissue paper and mints, if desired.

How-To Section

If there's something about the patterns, sewing or embroidery stitches that you don't understand, look it up here. Please read the complete instructions for each project before cutting your materials because there may be exceptions to these rather general directions.

Supplies and Tools

You'll need shears and scissors for cutting paper, cardboard and fabric. You can also make good use of a small hobby knife with a sharp point, such as the X-acto knife with #11 blade. It's ideal for cutting out stencil details in paper and cardboard. You can make do with a single-edge razor blade, but an X-acto is safer and much easier to use.

A wise investment will be a pair of lightweight embroidery scissors. The ones I purchased have plastic contour handles and very sharp, tapered stainless steel points. They're excellent for precision cutting of felt shapes and for clipping into small V areas of fabric.

Pinking shears are also good to have on hand, but only one project in the book (the cactus pincushion) actually requires them. When trimming seams, pinking shears often eliminate time-consuming clipping of curves.

Transparent tracing paper is a must for copying patterns. Dressmaker's carbon and a tracing wheel will be useful, if you have them. You'll want a soft pencil, a ball-point pen and a soft white drawing pencil (for marking dark colors).

A ruler is necessary for tracing straight lines; if it's metal, you can also use it as a cutting edge with your X-acto knife. Also helpful: tape measure; yardstick; T-square, triangle or right angle for making perfect 90° corners; and a compass for drawing accurate circles.

Some designs call for bonding two materials together. You can use fusible web on almost all fabrics; follow package directions for applying heat. If you're layering felt, use a thin coat of white glue or rubber cement, or the fusible web.

Along with threads and yarns to match your fabrics, you'll need pins and a selection of needles, some with large eyes for yarn embroidery and sturdy ones for sewing through latex-backed carpeting.

Polyester quilt batting comes in several thicknesses, and you can substitute multiple thin layers for one thick layer, if necessary. Save all the scraps for stuffing small toys. If a project requires a small amount of batting and you don't have any on hand, remember that it can be purchased in a crib-quilt size—you don't have to buy a huge bed-size!

An iron is an essential piece of equipment for me. I advise pressing each seam as you finish stitching it. A small tailor's ham is handy for pressing curved seams.

As for turning and stuffing fabrics, use what's handy. I find a crochet hook almost invaluable for turning legs and arms of small dolls, and a long ruler or wooden spoon handle is equally handy for turning straps. You'll need a yardstick, café curtain rod or dowel for turning the long tubes of the wall lion's braided mane.

Making Patterns

Most of the patterns in this book are actual-size, ready for you to trace. Two designs are drawn on grids and need to be enlarged (directions follow). In a few cases, you will have to draw squares, rectangles or circles.

The best paper for pattern-

Figure 1 *Enlarging a pattern.*

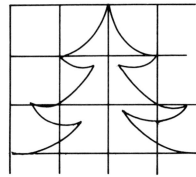

129

making is transparent tracing paper from art supply stores— it's available in tablets or by the roll. The 36″ roll is wide enough to make any pattern in this book.

To enlarge a pattern, rule your paper with squares (dimensions for squares are given with individual patterns). Copy pattern outline from the small squares to the corresponding large squares, as in Figure 1.

(You can buy large printed sheets of graph paper in stationery stores to make drawing the large squares easier. But graph paper is rather expensive, and relying on it can be inconvenient, especially if you're like me and start projects long after most stores have closed for the night.)

When you enlarge patterns or trace actual-size patterns from the book, always draw all the features, matching dots, etc., and label each piece. This can save you many frustrating moments later.

In trying to fit full-size patterns on the book pages, I've broken some patterns into pieces. Directions are given for butting these pieces together to make the complete pattern outline.

Where both sides of a pattern are identical, sometimes I've drawn only half the pattern. When you trace this, use folded tracing paper; lay the paper fold on the "place on fold" edge of the pattern. Cut out the paper, unfold it and you have the full-size pattern.

Felt

Since felt has no grain, you can lay out pattern pieces any which way, like a jigsaw puzzle, to conserve material. If the felt is creased, steam-press before cutting—it shrinks. Do not wash felt articles; dry clean only.

A few patterns call for felt cutouts of double thickness. Brush felt sparingly with white glue or rubber cement and press two layers together; let dry, then cut out pieces. (If using rubber cement, apply to both felt surfaces,

130

and allow to dry before joining.)

You can also use fusible web between layers, but it tends to make the felt rather stiff.

Other Fabrics

Use lightweight fabrics (broadcloth weight) for small items like the doll's clothing, and for most appliqués. If fabric is too heavy or stiff, it's difficult to turn under seam allowances for appliqués, or to turn small items right side out after stitching.

Avoid fabrics that fray easily. When you look at loose openweave fabrics, it's usually apparent that fraying will be a problem, but sometimes it can happen with closely woven fabrics, too. To save yourself a lot of grief, always check and try to unravel a few threads of any fabric you've chosen.

Where the grain of fabric is important to the design, I've marked patterns to show straight-of-grain. Also included are cutting layouts for designs with many pieces.

Tracing Patterns on Fabric

When yardages are given, it is assumed that the fabric is at least 44″ wide unless otherwise specified. I don't allow much extra length when I list fabric requirements. That's because I lay out pieces very close together, with seam allowance edges touching at times. If this is "too close for comfort" for you, always buy a little extra. Or better yet, change your ways and begin to conserve!

Lay patterns face down on the wrong side of fabric and trace around them with a pencil or ball-point pen. If pattern outlines are stitching lines, leave at least ½″ between pieces to allow for seams. When cutting fabric, add ¼″ seam allowance unless otherwise specified. I use this method because I like to have the precise stitching line drawn on each fabric piece.

If pattern outlines are cutting lines (usually with felt appliqués

or with edges to be bound), pattern pieces can be placed closer together on fabric.

When you will be using patterns more than two or three times, glue or trace them onto lightweight cardboard and cut them out.

Transferring Embroidery Details to Fabric

There are several ways to mark the right side of fabrics for embroidery and placement of appliqués. Choose the one best suited to your fabric—and your standards.

I'm fussy about pencil lines showing on the face of fabric. So if I'm working on light colors, I trace the design lightly on the wrong side, then baste along the tracing line to get the pattern outline on right side of fabric.

If the pattern is on tracing paper, you can go over the line on the back of the paper with soft pencil, lay the pattern on the right side of the fabric and rub off the design with your fingernail or a blunt tool. Or you can use dressmaker's carbon and a tracing wheel to transfer the outlines of large details.

The rub-off technique and dressmaker's carbon do not always leave clear pattern outlines on felt. The best way to mark felt is to punch through the tracing paper with a fat needle, then use a ball-point pen or pencil to make dots along the detail lines. On dark felt, use a sharp-pointed white drawing pencil.

Another technique for transferring details is to cut the interior designs (eyes, smiles, etc.) and use the pattern like a template or stencil to draw lines on fabric. In most cases, I think it's best to embroider facial features after you stuff a toy, because stuffing can distort a face so much. You may even prefer to wait and transfer the features after stuffing. Draw the face on tracing paper, make a template and find the best position for it on the head.

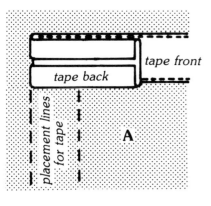

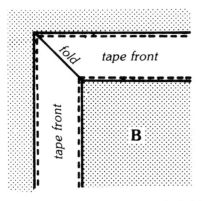

Figure 2 *Mitering single-fold bias tape used as a flat trim.*

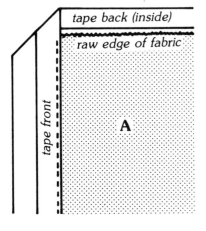

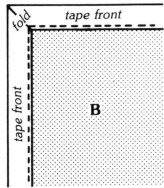

Figure 3 *Mitering double-fold bias tape used as a binding.*

Appliqués

Before cutting out appliqué pieces, decide whether you will attach them by hand or by zig-zag stitching on your machine. If you use the machine, cut fabric on pattern outlines— without seam or hem allowance. Use fusible web to attach the cutout to fabric; then secure the edges with close zigzag stitches.

You can do more of your sewing in your lap (as take-along projects) if you attach appliqués by hand. Cut out designs, adding ¼" seam or hem allowance. Turn edges under and hold them under by finger-pressing, pressing with an iron or basting.

To help you handle small pieces easily, especially small circles, machine-stitch or hand-stitch on the tracing lines before cutting them out. This gives you a precise folding edge. Cut out pieces, adding ¼" seam allowance; clip or trim seam allowance as you turn under raw edges.

Better yet, cut circles with pinking shears—pinking trims out some of the bulk so edges turn under smoothly.

Pin appliqué cutouts to body fabric and baste in place. (If you don't baste the seam allowance when you turn it under, this basting will catch it.) Secure appliqués with blind hemming (invisible stitches) and/or with embroidery. I edge most of my appliqués with blanket stitches.

Stitching and Stuffing

I recommend pinning and basting pieces together before sewing. This is time-consuming, but the results are well worth the extra effort.

To make seams smooth on the right side, it is often necessary to trim and clip them. With bulky seams, I "grade" or "layer" the seam allowance, cutting away each separate layer at a different distance from the stitching line. For instance, if the seam is ½" wide, my first trim line for the bottom layer might be ⅜"

and the next ¼". If there is a third layer, such as batting, it would be trimmed to ⅛". This trims away much of the bulk and makes a neater finish.

At corners, trim close to the stitching, cutting across the corners. On curves, make vertical cuts into the seam allowance, almost to the stitching line.

When bias tape is used, it usually is mitered at corners. To miter single-fold bias tape used as a trim, refer to Figure 2. First, stitch tape in a straight line just to the turning point, covering adjoining placement lines. At corner, fold tape back so fold is even with outside placement line (Figure 2-A). Then fold tape down along placement lines to form the miter (Figure 2-B).

To miter double-fold bias tape used as a binding, see Figure 3. First, position cut edge of fabric inside tape. Fold tape onto fabric along one straight edge and baste or stitch (Figure 3-A). Then fold tape over fabric on adjoining edge to form the miter (Figure 3-B). Repeat on reverse side of fabric to miter other half of tape.

To quilt fabric layers, sew directly on top of the seam line, using thread to match or blend with the fabric. Catch all layers with each stitch. For hand quilting, use a small running stitch. For machine quilting, use a long straight machine stitch.

If you baste or gather on the machine, set the machine for a long stitch and loose tension. Then pull the bobbin thread, either to gather the fabric, or to remove the basting threads after the seam is finally completed.

When you use stuffing, insert very small quantities at a time. Start with the arms, legs and head (the "far away" areas). Use the blunt end of a crochet hook and really pack it in. You'll almost always use more stuffing than you estimate, so have an extra bag on hand. Sometimes I suggest maintaining a flat, softly stuffed appearance, but usually

131

it's best to stuff firmly.

One word of caution: Please avoid the use of buttons, bells, fringe balls and other "munchies" if there is a young child in the family who will receive one of your handmade gifts. Even if the item is not intended for the little one, the present often receives a thorough inspection by small curious hands.

Embroidery Stitches

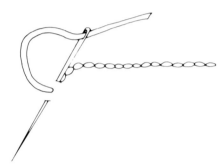

Backstitch. Work from right to left. Bring needle up on guideline. Take a stitch to the right, bringing needle up an equal distance ahead. Insert needle again at beginning of last stitch.

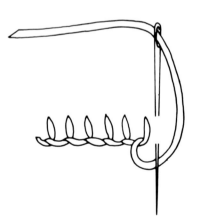

Blanket Stitch. Work from left to right (or top to bottom). Imagine two parallel lines. Bring needle out on bottom line; hold thread down with thumb. Insert needle above starting point and to the right; bring needle out again on lower line, drawing it over the loop of thread.

Buttonhole Stitch. Work exactly like blanket stitch, but keep stitches close together.

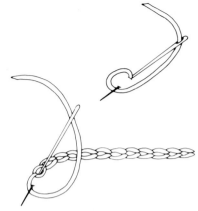

Chain Stitch. Work from top down (or right to left). Bring needle and thread to front. Make a loop with thread and hold it on fabric with left thumb. Insert needle again, as close as possible to where thread first came up. Take a short stitch ahead, drawing needle over loop.

Lazy Daisy Stitch. Make first loop as for the chain stitch. Insert needle to anchor loop and bring needle up at beginning of next loop.

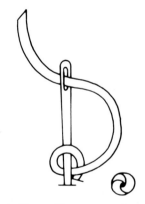

French Knot. Bring needle out where you want embroidered dot. Wrap thread two or three times around point of needle. Insert needle close to spot where thread emerged. Hold knot in place with left thumb and pull thread to wrong side.

Running Stitch. Work from right to left. Make stitches all the same size, with even spaces between stitches. Use this for quilting, gathering several stitches on your needle before pulling the thread through.

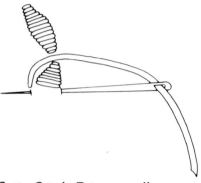

Satin Stitch. Bring needle up on left guideline. Insert on right guideline, carry thread behind work, and come up again on first guideline. Keep stitches smooth and close together; keep each stitch parallel to the preceding stitch.